When
Good
Things
Become
Addictions

D0376893

When Good Things Become Addictions

formerly titled <u>Regaining</u> <u>Control</u>

DR. GRANT MARTIN

VICTOR BOOKS®

A DIVISION OF SCRIPTURE PRESS PUBLICATIONS INC.
USA CANADA ENGLAND

For all illustrations used in this book which are taken
from true case histories, names, gender, and other
identifying information have been changed to protect
the actual people involved.

Unless otherwise indicated, Scripture quotations are
from the *Holy Bible, New International Version,*
© 1973, 1978, 1984, International Bible Society. Used
by permission of Zondervan Bible Publishers. Other
quotations are from the *Authorized (King James) Version* (KJV).

Recommended Dewey Decimal Classification: 200.19
Suggesteed Subject Heading: RECOVERY

ISBN: 0-89693-933-2

4 5 6 7 8 9 10 11 Printing/Year 95 94 93 92

CONTENTS

PREFACE

This book is about both powerlessness and hope. It is about the progressive loss of control over things that start out being healthy and good. Who could argue about the value of love, romance, relationships, food, success, physical fitness, and spiritual interests? Yet the harsh reality is that millions of Christians have lost their ability to manage significant parts of their lives. Much has been written about the destructive effects of alcohol and substance abuse. And, indeed, the consequences of drug and alcohol addiction are horrible and enormous. However, in Christian circles we don't see much written on the equally devastating effects of the addictions as presented in this book. My goal is to educate and awaken the Christian community to the facts of addictive behavior that might well affect all of us to one degree or another. Some may joke about being a workaholic or addicted to TV soap operas. These, and other forms of addictions, can lead to a sense of powerlessness, shame, and self-destruction every bit as harmful as booze and cocaine.

This book is also about hope. Before you regain control, you must come to a realization that you are out of control. That knowledge is the beginning of recovery. There are ways to overcome the powerlessness that accompanies addictive acting out. I am not promising easy solutions or quick cures. Recovery from any addiction takes time and hard work. But you can find some concrete guidelines in the pages to follow. We will be examining addiction in the areas of romance, relationships, sex, eating, power, religion, and activities.

Yes, even Christians can lose control of their lives. But with God's help and the honest admission of your needs, there can be a full and complete recovery. Whether you are concerned for yourself or someone you love, my prayer is that this book will speak to your needs and bring you to a fuller appreciation of God's grace and His power to restore.

Grant L. Martin, Ph.D.
Seattle, Washington
1990

To Jack L. Willcuts,
mentor and Quaker statesman,
who with humor and insight
encouraged and guided my early efforts in writing.
I am indebted to Uncle Jack
for his profound assistance.

CHAPTER ONE

INTRODUCTION TO ADDICTIONS
How Do We Get Hooked?

● "I can't help it," sobbed Emily. "I've tried dozens of diets, and lost hundreds of pounds in my life. But every time, I gain it all back, and sometimes more. I'd give anything to be slim. I hate myself. I'm fat. I'm depressed. And I guess I always will be."

Betty confessed, "I don't know what comes over me, but sometimes I get this compelling urge to buy things I don't even need and can't really afford. For a while it makes me feel good; but by the time I get home, I feel so guilty I'm sick. Then I tell myself, 'It will never happen again.' But it does. I just can't help it! I'm almost out of control."

"War on drugs!" leaps out from the headlines. The picture of a heroin addict injecting liquified powder into a pock-marked arm accompanies the narrative. "Hooked on chocolate," giggles the schoolgirl walking out of the candy store. One incident seems fatal, the other frivolous. The truth is that addictive behavior does not come in clearly marked gradations from safe to serious. Whatever the focus, addiction means you are out of control. You just can't help it.

Have you found yourself doing things you know you will later regret? Have you ever had the compelling urge to feel wonderful or to get rid of pain? To one degree or another, almost all of us could answer yes to these questions. It is possible that overeaters, heroin users, sky divers, abusive husbands, and lovers are driven by a similar compulsion.

The term *addiction* used to be reserved for a dependence on drugs. That may bring to mind images of drug addicts slumped over a syringe in a dingy doorway of a darkened alley. Or you may think of an alcoholic staggering down the sidewalk, panhandling for money to buy another bottle of Thunderbird. There are other addictions—romance, sex, food, power, relationships, or exercise. Most of us have lost at least a few battles with compelling urges.

This book will apply the principles of addiction to a range of compulsive behaviors as different as viewing pornography or eating too much chocolate. There are some essential chemical, psychological, and social common denominators between all forms of habitual behaviors. Whether your pleasure is scuba diving or jogging, shopping or sex, you are addicted if you cannot control when you start or stop it.

One of the key determinants in addiction is persistence. You continue with the behavior in spite of harmful consequences. However wonderful the feeling of the moment, the consequences of compulsive pleasure-seeking are often devastating and defeating. Yet, in spite of the cost, countless men and women have spent much of their lives in relentless pursuit of those transient moments of heavenly delight. If you are one of these people, or are concerned for someone else who has uttered the plea, "I can't help it!" I believe the material in this book will help you regain control.

Let's first examine what factors enter into the formation of addictive behavior. We are looking for the common threads that run through all types of compulsions.

ADDICTION IS A PROCESS
Addiction has been described in many ways. It has been called a disease, a moral weakness, lack of willpower, and sin. While there is an element of truth to each of these ideas, the point for right now is that addiction is a process. Addiction seldom remains constant. As it changes, it usually takes more and more of a person's energy and resources, to the point that it can become destructive and even fatal. Addiction is a set of experiences that produces changes within the person. The addict, responding to these internal changes, will begin to act out in particular ways. As addiction develops, it becomes a way of life. Since there are common patterns in this progression, we can use these characteristics to serve as bench marks of the addictive process.

To understand addiction we need to remember something very basic about human nature. We tend to want to do things that are rewarding and positive, and we tend to avoid things which are negative and aversive. If it hurts, we try to stop the pain. If it feels good, we want to do it again. If the conditions of the Garden of Eden were still in effect, there would be no addiction. The reason? Because there would be continual contentment, and no beginning for pain.

However, we live in a world where there are cycles of feeling. We desire to feel happy and to experience peace of mind. Sometimes we are able to experience pleasure. But it can't last forever. Life is not a constant mountaintop existence. The good feelings seem to slip away. When they leave, we may grieve, feel sad, or become depressed over the loss. On the other hand, it is just as inevitable that pain, hurt, or other negative experiences will enter our lives. It is inevitable that we will lose a loved one, suffer a loss of status, have a dream or ideal shattered, experience an end of a friendship, or have a prayer that seems unanswered in the way we want. These are the times when a person is susceptible to forming an addictive relationship.

Because we want to escape pain, we seek out objects or experiences that maximize the positive and eliminate the negative. There is a certain element of control we can exert in helping these cycles along, but the ups and downs are unavoidable. Since we cannot totally control the cycle of peace and pain, we must learn to either accept these cycles or try to be happy all of the time. The addict tries to control these uncontrollable events. When he engages in a particular object or event to produce a desired mood change, he believes he can control the cycle. The addict believes he can make the pain go away and bring about good feelings whenever he wants. And in the beginning he can be successful. But this is where the process becomes progressive. Just as cancer is a process involving the uncontrolled multiplying of harmful cells, addiction is the out-of-control search for either happiness or the avoidance of pain. Regardless of the addiction, every addict has a relationship with an object or event in order to produce a mood change.

- The compulsive spender seeks a mood change by going on a shopping spree.
- The sex addict seeks a mood change by seducing a partner.
- The food addict seeks a mood change by eating a gallon of ice cream or starving himself.

- The religious addict seeks a mood change by attending a church service for the purpose of getting a "spiritual high."
- The romance addict experiences a mood change by reading a spicy romance novel.

Each of the events is different. But the common goal for each addict is to produce a mood change. The means by which the mood change is accomplished is called *acting out*. When a sex addict looks for a prostitute, a shopper impulsively buys something he doesn't need, or an overeater binges on a gallon of ice cream, they are acting in such a way as to create a mood change. By acting out in either thought or action, the addict attempts to create feelings of relaxation, excitement, or fantasy. The change in mood resulting from the acting out gives the addict the illusion of being in control. The process continues as addicts attempt to make sense out of life. They believe they are being fulfilled by their behavior. Because the activity gains access to rewarding feelings, or at least helps escape pain and hurt, the process is reinforced. As the addictive cycle continues, the acting out behavior is also a way to escape the shame and guilt created by knowing that they are out of control.

SEDUCTIVE NATURE OF ADDICTION
As the addict continues to engage in the behavior, a very seductive thing happens. The addict begins to believe that he can be nurtured by objects or events. This happens because the acting out, whether relaxing, thrill seeking, or fantasy, allows the addict to get temporary relief from the pain and pressure of life. There is some short-term gain in having access to this mood-altering experience. We have all avoided dealing with some of life's unpleasant activities. As I write this chapter, my income tax forms have not been completed. I would much rather write about addiction than fill out my 1040 IRS form. But sometime before April 15, I will get it done.

The difference is that an addiction becomes a lifestyle in which the addict loses control and becomes enmeshed into a habitual avoidance of reality. Addicts try to nurture themselves by avoiding responsibility and denying reality. But in this process, the mood change created by the acting out creates an illusion of being nurtured.[1]

The workaholic spends 100 hours a week at the office, demands that her subordinates sacrifice weekends with their families, and grumbles about their level of commitment when they complain about the work load. While immersing herself in work, to avoid feelings of isolation, she maintains the illusion of close relationships with her coworkers. The work addiction provides the illusion of being comforted.

The food addict binges after a fight with her husband. For a short time she feels content and comfortable. The food has altered her mood, and she no longer feels empty and alone. The acting out with food has given her the feeling of being nurtured. For a few precious moments she feels in control.

Likewise, the shopping addict, while depressed over the lack of money to meet daily living expenses, will go out and buy a $200 water ski. It doesn't make logical sense, but it gives temporary relief from depression.

Gradually, seductively, the addict begins to depend on the addictive process for a sense of nurturing. She looks to the mood change to define who she is. The acting out helps avoid the negative feelings. Life takes on a singular focus — the pursuit of the addiction. This is part of the insanity of the addictive process. The addict is hoping to get her needs met by developing a relationship with an object or experience. Normally, people get emotional needs met by reaching out to other people. We establish intimate relationships with family, people in the community, our church, and God. The addict, with her singular focus, tends to withdraw and isolate herself. As this process continues, the addict feels even more hopeless about her ability to ever have a meaningful relationship with anyone outside of her addictive experience. The addict hurts; she is lonely and isolated. Others might reach out to a friend, talk to a spouse, call a parent, or pray. But the addict will turn to her addiction for relief. This subsequent mood change will then give the illusion that a need has been met; but she has been nurtured by the object or experience, not by the compassion of a loved one.

The problem with this aspect of the addictive process is that other people become singular objects for the addict to manipulate. The romance addict is enamored with the idea of being in love, not with the person. The sex addict sees his date as a sexual object first, and as a person second. The workaholic gets more out of using others to increase productivity at the office, than from developing friends among his coworkers. This misuse of people leads to greater isolation. The feelings of detachment and separation will only drive the addict into greater reliance on his mood-altering object or experience. It turns into a vicious cycle, and often leads to calamity and self-destruction.

Another reason the addict becomes separated from people is the reliability of objects. If you take a drug, you are practically guaranteed a mood change. Parachuting out of an airplane will almost always bring an adrenaline rush. Eating half a dozen doughnuts is likely to produce a temporary calming. For the addict, the object or experience can be trusted to provide a change in mood. People aren't so predictable; sometimes they let you down or are not there when you need them. As a result, the addict learns to trust his addiction more than people. It may seem crazy to an outsider, but it makes perfect sense to the addict. By acting out, the addict experiences a sense of control. This helps to counteract the feelings of powerlessness deep within. The promise of power in the face of helplessness is the nature of addiction. The addict begins to believe false and empty promises: the promise of relief, the promise of emotional security, the false sense of fulfillment, and the false sense of intimacy with the world.[2]

Certainly there is a biochemical basis to addictions. The discovery in 1974 of enkephalins by Jon Hughes and Hans Kosterlitz greatly expanded our understanding of human compulsions. Enkephalins, and related compounds called endorphins, are pain-killing molecules that are produced naturally in the brain. The strong mood-altering chemicals are structurally similar to opiate drugs and appear to behave in similar ways. The brain can actually produce its own opiates. Individuals can change their brain chemistry by participating in certain mood-altering activities, as well as through ingesting intoxicating substances. Leaping from an airplane and then free-falling from an altitude of 13,000 feet will produce a chemical change in the brain that is quite similar to taking a hit of cocaine.

While interesting and helpful, the chemical explanations for addiction are still not sufficient in and of themselves. Addictive behavior has its roots in every aspect of our being. That is why it is so seductive and compelling.

Addiction is evident when one becomes progressively unable to control the beginning or end of a need-fulfilling activity. Compulsive behavior is best understood as an individual's self-defeating adjustment to his environment. It represents an habitual style of coping. But it is a style of coping that can be altered. We are not locked into a fixed pattern of behavior from which there is no escape. There is hope, even though the pathway to recovery is narrow and long. It is possible to regain control.

ADDICTIVE THINKING

What we believe is very important. Beliefs determine action. Beliefs are like road maps, signs, and laws of the highway. They tell us where to go, how to get there, and how we should behave on the way. While often outside of our conscious awareness, beliefs have a direct bearing on what we do. The Bible validates our common experience when it teaches, "For as he thinketh in his heart, so is he" (Proverbs 23:7, KJV). Our actions follow from what we believe to be true. The feelings and actions of the addict are affected by certain beliefs about events and situations. Many of those beliefs may not be true, but they are held to tenaciously, because the addict knows no other way.

On a logical level, addicts know that an object or event cannot bring emotional fulfillment. Alcoholics know they can't escape into a bottle. Addictive spenders know that money can't buy happiness. But addiction does not follow usual logic. It does make sense, however, when viewed through the eyes of the addicts. Emotional intimacy, whether positive or negative, is experiential and is not a product of conscious, logical thought. Emotional needs are often urgent and compulsive. Emotions say, "I want it now!" Addicts try to satisfy their urgently felt need as quickly as possible, even when it is not in their best interests.

When a sex addict feels depressed, he rents an x-rated video, and feels better for a short time. Since the good feelings don't last, he will probably feel guilty and remorseful the next morning. The thinking of an addict is often divided. Part of the sex addict's thinking said that the movie would take his mind off of his problems. Another part reminded him of his promise to his wife not to view this material again. But his wife is out of town and the emotional pressure is building. He wants the stimulation of the movie, so he finally gives in to the emotional logic that says the mood-altering experience of watching an x-rated movie will make him feel better. He is doing something to make himself feel good, and he is doing it now. How could the logic be better? See how addictions can be cunning, baffling, and powerful?[3]

The verse from Proverbs 23 cited earlier actually occurs in the context of cautioning against addictive behavior. Here more of that passage encourages temperate behavior.

Do not crave his delicacies, for that food is deceptive. Do not wear yourself out to get rich; have the wisdom to show restraint. Cast but a glance at riches, and they are gone, for they will surely sprout wings and fly off to the sky like an eagle. Do not eat the food of a stingy man, do not crave his delicacies; for he is the kind of man who is always thinking about the cost. "Eat and drink," he says to you, but his heart is not with you (Proverbs 23:3-7).

Notice how food, money, delicacies, and drink have become the object of attention to the exclusion of people. " 'Eat and drink,' he says to you, but his heart is not with you." Doesn't this sound like an addict? It's not the people he cares about, but the mood-altering object or experience. The belief system is saying, "The only way to get my needs met is by excessive consumption." This is an illustration of the ageless nature of faulty thinking in the addictive cycle.

A person's belief system will influence whether he will continue to return to an experience that is progressively damaging. Even after an addictive attachment has developed, a person can choose to change his belief system to either support or reject the addiction. Thus, understanding our beliefs, both true and false, is a vital component in understanding the causes and providing relief from the addiction. An important part of the subsequent chapters on the specific addictive patterns will be the description of the typical thought patterns that accompany the behavior.

STAGES OF ADDICTION
There are three stages to the addiction process. The first involves internal changes. The personality begins to change as a result of the intoxicating experiences. The second stage involves changes in lifestyle. Now it is more obvious to those around the addict because he is behaving in ways that are unusual and counterproductive. The final stage occurs

when the addict becomes out of control. Nothing matters but getting more of the mood-altering experience. Pleasure is gone and life is only a survival ordeal. Here are some of the details of each stage.

Stage One. A winning bet pays off big. The compulsive purchase of an unnecessary item helps to appease a downcast feeling. An emotion-filled church service brings about feelings of joy and exhilaration. All of these events could be the start of an addictive journey. For the addict, a life experience that produces a pleasurable mood change can give the illusion of control and comfort. The initial experiences are usually quite intoxicating. This *euphoric experience* teaches the prospective addict that one's feelings can change through a relationship with an object or event. This intense feeling, unfortunately, gets mistaken for intimacy, nurturance, and a sense of personal power.

Addiction begins when a person repeatedly seeks the illusion of relief to avoid unpleasant feelings or situations. Emotional needs are met by seeking nurturing through avoidance. Family, friends, church, and God begin to be given up as a source of emotional relief or support and the addict seeks out an object or experience for his serenity. Nakken describes the addictive cycle shown in Figure 1, beginning with the experience of pain (A). The person wants to avoid the pain, so feels the need to soothe the pain (B). This urge leads to (C) acting out, and the resulting mood change. The person starts to feel better. But pretty quickly there is the pain resulting from acting out (D). Now the person has experienced pain again (A), so feels the need to act out again (B), does act out (C), feels pain and remorse (D), and the cycle goes on and on (ABCD, ABCD, ABCD, etc.).

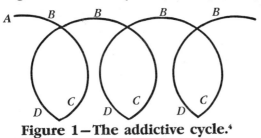

Figure 1 – The addictive cycle.[4]

At this point the addiction starts to create the very thing the person is trying to avoid — pain. However, in creating pain, the process also creates a need for the continuation of the addictive relationship. The addict seeks refuge from the pain of addiction by moving further into the addiction.

This cycle causes an emotional craving that results in mental *preoccupation*. The feelings of discomfort and pain become a signal to act out. A healthy reaction to stress or discomfort is to reach out to family, friends, community, or God. The addict reaches out to the mood-altering experience instead. The more ingrained the cycle, the greater the preoccupation and dependency. Nakken makes the point that eventually the person forms a *dependent relationship* with his own addictive personality.[5]

Once an addictive personality is established, the specific object or event takes on less importance. This means the addict can switch objects of addiction. The overeater can diet, refrain from binging, but start shopping. The impulse spending may go away, but the exhilarating feelings from making an important business decision may take on greater power to help avoid the pain. Addicts who switch objects of addiction also know that the switch is a good way to get people off of their backs.

The bottom line for the recovering addict is to understand that the addictive personality will stay with him for life. At some level, his personality will always be looking for an object or experience to give him the illusion of nurturing. A common statement from a dry or nondrinking alcoholic is, "I now overeat for the same reasons I drank: I'm lonely and afraid." Often the thing that stands in the way of recovery is another addiction. And the major reason is that the person has become controlled by an addictive personality even without the initial object being present.

Stage Two. Addictive behavior such as overspending, viewing x-rated movies, or binging, occurs regularly once the addictive personality has developed. The acting out is a sign that the person is out of control on an internal level. In Stage Two, the person becomes out of control on a behavioral level.[6]

In Stage Two the episodes of being *behaviorally out of control* become more frequent. The addict becomes more preoccupied with the object or event that can temporarily stop the pain. At this stage *others start to notice* something is wrong. Coworkers, family, and friends begin to see the presence of an addictive personality.

In Stage One a person usually acts within socially acceptable limits. In Stage Two she starts to act out her belief system in a ritualistic manner and her behavior is more out of control. She becomes dependent on the addictive personality, not just the mood change or the object or event. The addictive belief system develops into a *lifestyle.*

In this stage the person uses *addictive logic* to guide the arrangement of her life and relationships. The behavioral commitment to the addictive process is all-encompassing.[7] Here are some of the ways this stage shows itself:

- The addict lies when it would be easier to tell the truth.
- The person blames others, knowing it is not true.
- Behavior becomes ritualized.
- The person withdraws from others.
- The food addict starts to hide food or starves herself.
- The romance addict hoards romance novels by the dozens.
- The sex addict goes to prostitutes or has multiple affairs.
- The addictive spender will open secret bank accounts or get a secret job to cover his losses.
- The religious addict will attend numerous churches searching for new euphoric experiences.

Each of these examples demonstrates a behavioral commitment to the addictive process. Every time the addict acts out, she is depending more on the addictive personality and less on herself and others who love her. Because the addict must make emotional sense to herself of the inappropriate behavior, she turns to *denial,* repression, lies, rationalizations, and other defenses to cope with what is happening.

When the addict acts out and then explains it away, he deepens his commitment to addiction. When the addict acts out, he must withdraw into his addictive personality to receive support. This action causes him to become even more *isolated* from others around him. This creates feelings of loneliness and a desire to reach out and connect. But because reaching out to family or friends is frightening, the loneliness becomes another signal to act out. This vicious cycle serves to strengthen the addictive process.

In Stage Two the behavior of the addict becomes more *ritualized.* The purpose of a ritual is to act out with the body what one thinks in his brain. When the addict engages in ritualistic behavior, he is making a behavioral statement that supports the addictive process and belief system. For example, the act of attending a family birthday party makes a statement in support of one's family and the family's belief system. For the addict, a ritual brings a form of comfort because it is predictable. A particular sequence of behavior becomes conditioned or associated with a mood change. The sex addict may dress in certain clothes and cruise particular streets in his search for stimulation. The food addict may use a ritual of preparing certain foods, watching TV, or eating and reading after the evening meal as his way of avoiding pain. In each case the ritual becomes valuable to the addict because it is connected with the feeling in which he has found at least some short-term comfort.

Healthy rituals serve to bind us to family and friends. Addictive rituals serve to isolate the addict from others. Healthy rituals help us feel better about ourselves. Addictive rituals make the addict feel worse about himself. Healthy rituals help us have better relationships. Addictive rituals destroy relationships. Healthy rituals help us feel pride about ourselves and others. Addictive rituals cause shame.[8]

In Stage Two the person tries to establish behavioral limits, but it doesn't work. The addict believes he should be able to control the addictive behavior. Each time he acts out, his internal self feels more shame. In Stage Two he eventually *surrenders* to the immense power of addiction.

As the addict becomes more controlled by the process, those people around the addict sense his emotional withdrawal and react to it. This is the start of *people problems,* as the addict manipulates people and treats them as objects. The concern of others is seen by the addict as an invasion of privacy. If family or friends try to help and find out what is happening, they will be met with resistance in the form of a lie, silent withdrawal, or an attack.

In Stage Two the addict projects his beliefs and values on everyone else. Since he believes people are objects to be manipulated, he suspects everyone else is doing the same thing. As a result he feels victimized and looks for someone to blame. That villain is usually someone close, such as a spouse or parent. The next thing that happens is for the people around the addict to *label* the addict as irresponsible, troubled, tense, crazy, or strange. This may be done with phrases such as, "He's a bum!" "She eats too much!" "All he does is spend, spend, spend!" "All she does is work!" "He's obsessed with sex!" or "He'll do anything for a thrill!"

When labeling takes place, it's a sign that addiction has progressed to the point that family and friends are noticing something is wrong. Labeling is an attempt to control what is happening. Often the addict becomes a *scapegoat* to take the blame for everything bad that happens. He will likely react and try to protect himself. In doing so the addictive defense system will become even better developed.

Another thing that happens as a result of labeling is the *self-fulfilling prophecy.* As the negative labels are applied to the addict and the role of scapegoat is assigned, the addictive personality finds more freedom to act irresponsibly. "People think I'm a bum, so I might as well act like one." "I'm a fat slob, so why not go ahead and eat. Nobody cares about me anyway." "So what if I spend too much money. That's what people expect me to do, so I won't let them down." In this way, the addict gives himself permission to act out as a result of being labeled.

Over time addicts adjust to the mood change produced by their acting out. As a result they must act out more frequently and with greater intensity. Stage Two includes the development of a *tolerance.* Because of this tolerance and the increased anger and pain, the addict will start to act out more frequently and in more dangerous ways. Overeaters may binge more often, but start using laxatives to keep from gaining weight. The relationship addict may strive harder to pacify an abusive husband, even to the point of risking physical injury. The thrill addict may try more dangerous activities beyond what his skills would allow. This constant attempt to keep ahead of the tolerance level, combined with the internal emotional struggle, is a tremendous *energy drain.* Energy once directed toward family, friends, and self-care is now used to sustain the addiction. An internal struggle takes place. It consists of "Should I or shouldn't I?" The addict struggles with the desire to act out, and the possibility of getting into trouble. Like any progressive illness, the addiction will take more of the addict's energy and attention, limiting his ability to live a "normal" life.

The final characteristic of Stage Two is *spiritual deadening.* Connections with God, church, community, and fellowships become dull and meaningless. The soul seems bereft of any sense of God's nearness and has little appetite for Scripture, sermons, discussions, and prayer. The longer the addiction goes on the more spiritually isolated the person becomes. The addict feels out of control, has built up a tolerance, created a denial system, and is experiencing a great deal of anger and shame. At the very time the spiritual dimension is most needed, the addict is spiritually empty.

Stage Three. At this point the addict's life will start to break down under the tremendous stress caused by the increased pain, anger, and fear which results from continuously acting out.[9] By Stage Three the addictive personality is in total control. The only thing of importance to the addict is achieving and maintaining control over her ability to get high from acting out. At this point, acting out no longer produces much ecstasy. Preoccupation, rituals, and acting out will still produce a mood change, but the pain never goes away. The magical intoxication begins to break down under stress because the person is on a physical, emotional, social, and spiritual overload. The addict starts behaving in ways she never thought possible. The dangerous life-threatening aspects of the process become obvious to the addict and to her family and friends. One of the strong possibilities at this point is that she will become so totally committed to the addiction process that she will not be able to break the cycle. Only strong and appropriate intervention has a chance of making a difference.

In Stage Three the addict makes no attempt to make sense of her behavior. She falls into a lifestyle devoted to addictive ritual. Life is totally controlled by the addictive belief system. The logic of the addict is simple—"get high and exist." She is preoccupied with those things that will help her maintain the addictive lifestyle. Nothing else matters.[10]

In Stage Three the person's emotions start to break down. He may cry uncontrollably for the slightest reason, go into angry outrages or tantrums for seemingly no reason. Suspicion bordering on paranoia results from the attempt to defend himself from outside connections. Free-floating anxiety, panic attacks, and hysteria can strike and last for a few moments to several days. There is a feeling that the whole world has turned against him and that no one cares.

Up to now the addict has interacted with others by manipulating and using them to fulfill his addictive needs. In Stage Three he starts to *lose his effectiveness*. He is no longer able to manipulate so as to further his addictive lifestyle. Meanwhile family and friends are fed up. Many will have left or abandoned the addict. At this time the only persons who are around are those doing so out of feelings of responsibility, pity, or guilt. The addict now tries to get people to take care of him through emotional blackmail. He may threaten suicide or other consequences if his family or friends don't help out.

The Stage Three addict has become totally afraid of intimacy and stays away from any sign of it. She thinks others are the source of all her problems, so people are to be avoided. From one perspective she wants to be alone. However, at the same time, she craves emotional connection with others. Down deep she is deathly afraid of being alone. So while in one way she will go to great lengths to be alone, she will also attempt to connect with others by clinging to family or friends. With almost a childlike quality, the addict will become upset if it looks like people are withdrawing. She will want to know where the person is going when a family member leaves the house, for example. Phrases such as, "You can't leave me, you're all I have!" "Just one more chance, I promise I'll straighten up," are common for the addict. She behaves as if she is telling people to stay away, but when people do withdraw, she becomes quite upset.

Environmental problems abound at this stage. The addict's work is endangered, marriages are threatened or ended, financial problems are overwhelming or legal problems emerge. Physical problems also occur. The liver of the alcoholic, the gums of the bulimic, sexually transmitted diseases from sexual promiscuity, ulcers, high blood pressure, and heart attacks for the power addict, may all be consequences of years of a stress-filled lifestyle. The physical damage resulting from addiction is enormous, both for the addict and for his family and friends. Suicide is a common consideration at this stage. Depression, anger, rage, guilt, shame, loneliness, and hopelessness can combine to make the addict view self-destruction as the only viable alternative to escape the overwhelming pain.

Addicts cannot break the addictive process and will *remain stuck* in Stage Three unless there is some form of intervention. They must acknowledge that they are out of control, and then turn to the difficult task of learning a new lifestyle. That is why this book has been written—to help those who are caught in the web of self-destruction or who seek to intervene with a loved one who is out of control. Recovery is a difficult but possible goal with the love of God, and the help of family, friends, and a caring community.

We can suspect addiction if we see denial, immediate need, compulsion to act out, progression from one level to another, loss of control, and withdrawal symptoms. These key features will be described for each addiction.

THE ISSUE OF RESPONSIBILITY

You may have noticed I have refrained from using the terms disease or illness in my discussion of the addictive process. Is addiction a disease, a moral problem, sin, or a progression of choices? The answer to this question continues to generate a great deal of debate. I am reluctant to adopt the disease model as the sole explanation for a very complicated phenomenon. The addictive experience is the totality of all that a person is. There are chemical and physical contributions. But there are also important contributions from the person's cultural, spiritual, emotional, and social history. Within all of these factors, I believe there is a crucial place for personal choice and responsibility.

Some claim that the addict has no choice because the addiction is in charge. This presents a very deterministic view of the individual as having no control over his choices because of the presence of the addictive disease. The contradiction comes, however, when the addict is counseled that the very first step in recovery is to *choose* to admit that he is powerless and unable to manage or control his life. Why do we have laws against drinking to excess? If an alcoholic has a disease, in the medical sense, why do we prosecute for drunken driving or vehicular homicide? We don't take such action if a person passes out from an insulin reaction or a heart attack. Somehow the illness explanation is not totally sufficient for most addictive behavior.

The advantage of the disease model of addiction is that it allows insurance companies to pay for treatment; also it takes some of the stigma off of the person who abuses alcohol or substance. With the encouragement that the addict is not a bad person, but has inherited or developed an uncontrollable illness, many addicts have been able to admit to their problem and take the initial steps toward recovery. These would appear to be important gains, but the disease model does have its critics.[11]

One important consideration is the necessity to include the spiritual dimension in any discussion of change or recovery. If taken as a singular explanation, the disease approach could omit the spiritual. This argument might proceed as follows. A person inherits a predisposition to become addicted. The right combination of stress, opportunity, and repetitions results in the person acquiring the disease of alcoholism (or sex abuse, or bulimia, etc.).

A positive approach to addiction demands the inclusion of the spiritual aspect of humanity, and the importance of personal accountability. Addiction cannot be explained in singular terms. Even those who propose a disease-based explanation, when pressed, will acknowledge that addiction is not just a physical, but also a psychological, spiritual, and cultural problem. What happens is that medical terms are used without a precise understanding of the causation.

Addiction can certainly have a physiological component. If the explanation is made solely in terms of neurotransmitters and nerve cell interaction, those processes are certainly beyond our control. But we must be held responsible for how we act in response to those patterns.

A parallel example might be anger. The beginning stages of anger are automatic responses to perceived danger or threat. When a danger alert is transmitted to the brain from one of the five senses, a complex series of bodily reactions immediately takes place without conscious thought. Adrenaline pours into the bloodstream, heartbeat and blood pressure increase, more oxygen is supplied to the muscles and brain, and the pupils dilate, improving vision. All of this happens without our having to make any choices. Initially, there is no time for deliberate thought. Thus, we are not so much responsible for being in a state of anger, as we are accountable for what is done with our anger. Once the conscious mind takes over—and that may be only a few seconds—we are answerable for how we deal with the anger.

Within the addictive cycle there is always choice. While the existence of the compulsion is beyond our control, we can control how we respond to it. This is where the integration of choice and the spiritual dimension takes place. Without the grace of God we are, indeed, powerless. The Apostle Paul spoke to this very idea when he said, "I know that nothing good lives in me, that is, in my sinful nature. For I have the desire to do what is good, but I cannot carry it out" (Romans 7:18). Our competence comes only from God (2 Corinthians 3:5), but we must make the choice to seek His help and deliverance. (There will be a more detailed discussion of surrender in chapter 9.)

We must remember the insidious and progressive nature of addictions. It doesn't matter whether we are talking about sex, thrills, work, relationships, money, or power. The eventual lack of control, with its concomitant physical, emotional, social, intellectual, and spiritual facets, will eventuate in the addiction being the central activity in the person's life.

It is a fact that if you have spent months or years developing an addictive attraction, it is very difficult to make significant changes. Even if you "want to change," it is formidable. But you have to take the responsibility to start the journey.

My intent is to give compassion and concern to those struggling with self-control. To place a label of "sin," "disease," or "unwise choices" does not help. We must come alongside the addict, show compassion without becoming entangled in the web of deceit, and be firm and wise in our encouragement and guidance. It is not easy and there will undoubtedly be failures. Consistent balance is difficult: we don't want to encourage codependency on the one hand or selfish reclusiveness on the other. However, freedom, recovery, and serene sobriety are possible.

DIFFERENCES BETWEEN ADDICTION AND NONADDICTION

The fundamental distinction between addiction and non-addiction is between the desire to grow and the desire to remain dormant. The difference is one of seeing the world as an arena with opportunity for change and improvement, or seeing the world as your prison. When life is seen as an overwhelming burden, full of useless struggles against overpowering obstacles, addiction can be a way to surrender.

Evaluate your favorite experiences in light of the following questions.
• Does the experience enhance your ability to live?
• Does the experience help bond you to other people?
• Does it help you to bear fruit that encourages and builds up others?
• Does it enable you to work more effectively?
• Does it encourage you to love more beautifully?
• Does it bring you to a closer relationship with God?
• Does it permit you to appreciate the world around you more?

- Does it foster growth, change, and expansion?
- Does it facilitate the experience of joy and pleasure?
- Does it allow you to make choices?
- Does it allow you to control when you start and stop the activity?

If the answer to these questions is yes, the experience is not addictive. If you had several negative responses, you need to evaluate your experience. If an object or experience diminishes you, makes you less attractive, less capable, less sensitive, or limits, stifles, or harms, then it is addictive.

An experience can be intensely absorbing without being addictive. If you can engage in something from interest, curiosity, satisfaction, or sense of accomplishment, as opposed to seeking out its most superficial but pleasurable features, you are not addicted. Addiction is marked by an intensity of need in which a person pursues the sensual aspect of an experience, primarily for its intoxicating effects.

When someone has a healthy enjoyment for an experience, she wants to master or understand it better. The addict wishes to stay with a "safe," clearly defined routine. No emotional risk is involved. This perspective might suggest the dedicated artist, author, or scientist is addicted to his work, but this need not be so. What distinguishes intense concentration from addiction is that the intense scientist is not escaping from pain, isolation, novelty, and uncertainty into a predictable, comforting state of affairs. She receives the pleasure of creation and discovery from the activity. Sometimes that pleasure is deferred for a long time. The scientist moves on to new problems, sharpens her skills, takes risks, meets resistance and frustration, and challenges herself. Whatever personal incompleteness may exist does not diminish her integrity and capacity to live. The diligent scholar does not want to escape from herself. She is in touch with a difficult and demanding reality and her accomplishments will be evaluated by her peers. Finally they can be judged by the benefits they bring to the rest of humanity.

The ability to derive pleasure from a task, or to do something because it brings joy, is a criterion of nonaddiction. An addict does not take drugs for enjoyment but to obliterate dreaded aspects of the world. A cigarette addict or an alcoholic may once have enjoyed a smoke or a drink; but by the time he has become addicted, he is driven to use the substance merely to maintain a bearable level of existence. Because his entire system has undergone the tolerance process, the addict now needs the experience just for survival.

Likewise the compulsive eater is not particular about the type of food available, just that it is accessible. With many addictions, choices about the setting, risk, brand, style, cost, etc. are not really functional to the addict. A person addicted to a relationship which is abusive, for example, will continue with that alliance, having lost the ability to discriminate between the available options.

SUMMARY AND PREVIEW

I have tried to describe the addiction process with enough breadth so as to encompass all forms of compulsive behavior. While there are disadvantages in doing this, I hope the reader can get an idea of the nature, pattern, and progression of compulsive behavior.

The following chapters deal with particular types of addiction. In each chapter the behavior pattern will be described, and often will include self-tests and rating scales to help you identify your own status. Where appropriate, the stages and levels characteristic of that particular addiction will be given. Some of the key features of that compulsion will be presented, followed by suggestions for recovery.

There are no instant cures offered here; addiction is a complicated and serious problem. But God has told us we can be free as a result of knowing and abiding in His truth. May this material be helpful in your journey to freedom!

N O T E S

1. Craig Nakken, *The Addictive Personality* (San Francisco: Harper/ Hazelden), 1988, 7.
2. *Ibid.,* 14.
3. *Ibid.,* 9.
4. *Ibid.,* 24.
5. *Ibid.,* 24.
6. *Ibid.,* 24.
7. *Ibid.,* 37.
8. *Ibid.,* 46.
9. *Ibid.,* 55.
10. *Ibid.,* 56–57.
11. Herbert Fingarette, *Heavy Drinking: the Myth of Alcoholism as a Disease* (Berkeley: University of California Press), 1988.

CHAPTER TWO

ROMANCE ADDICTION
*Are You in Love
with the Idea of Love?*

● Paul is an attractive man in his mid-forties who lives for the romantic moments in his life. Paul didn't date much in high school, but when he went away to college he dated more frequently and became sexually active. He has had many partners, but is still uncomfortable with women. Paul spends much of his time fantasizing about his next sexual encounter. He likes to talk about his sexual relationships with the guys at the health club. While he gives off a confident air, he is lonely and depressed.

Shelly is married with two children and appears outwardly happy to her friends at church. She is thirty pounds overweight and has difficulty keeping up with her housework, but finds time every day to watch two or three of her favorite TV soap operas. Her closet is filled with dozens of romance novels, and she has rented almost every romantic movie at the local video store. Shelly feels guilty about her use of time, but just can't seem to get it under control.

Paul and Shelly are addicted because their lives are out of control. Addictive behavior can be found in almost any area of our lives, even our love life.

Professionals who have studied many types of addictions have reached a surprising conclusion. The addicting element is not so much a substance, such as cocaine or alcohol, but something within the person who is addicted. In romance addiction, this addictive element takes the form of a compelling need to maintain an illusion of being in love. This kind of addiction has nothing to do with love or commitment. Love is meant to be mutual and uplifting. Romance addiction is selfish and destructive.

TYPES OF "LOVE" ADDICTIONS

There has been a recent surge in attention to addictive behavior patterns other than those involving drugs and alcohol. Books have been written talking about codependence, love addiction, and addiction to a person. Anne Wilson Schaef has written an excellent book entitled *Escape from Intimacy* in which she proposes that sex, romance, and relationship addictions are separate addictions. She suggests that even those who may have fallen within the description of codependent probably have an undetected core addiction. I believe she is correct. Therefore, in this and the next two chapters, I will summarize the characteristics and levels of *romance, relationship,* and *sexual* addiction as separate and distinct types of love addictions.

Addictions tend to cluster. Several may be present in one person. Also it is important to remember addictions are progressive, and can be fatal. This means we must attempt to understand the underlying addictive process *together* and *separately* for recovery to take place.

ROMANCE ADDICTION

Romance junkies demand or beg for approval and affection in an escalating cycle of disappointment and reprisal. For them their addictive behavior makes perfect sense because it feels necessary to survival. To an addictive lover, a pathological relationship may seem normal and necessary. Eventually, harmful consequences result, including deterioration of work, social, or health functions.

Those who become addicted usually lack confidence in their ability to cope without some form of real or imagined support from a love object. This chronic and intense form of lovesickness is characterized by depression, depletion of energy, and change in appetite in response to feelings of rejection. On the other hand, when a romantic figure shows even minimal signs of approval, the lovesick person reacts with increased energy and euphoria out of proportion to the situation at hand.

The romance addict is in love with the idea of romance and lives a life of illusion. The romance addict believes that someday her prince will actually come. Often the fantasied focus of the addict's attention is unattainable. She is obsessed with the accoutrements of relationships, but not with the actual relationship. Romance addicts take the most vulnerable aspects of human interactions and feed their addiction.

It is difficult for addicts to form happy, committed relationships because they are terrified of intimacy. Their romantic attachment is no more than an object to provide the desired emotional fix. Romance addiction can be played out in relationships as well as in adventures or social and political causes. The important element is the thrill of the fix.

CHARACTERISTICS OF ROMANCE ADDICTION[1]

Dishonesty. The romance addict is concerned more with the setting than the person. He appears to be interested in the other person, but actually uses form as a fix. The goal is to experience the buzz of a new romantic experience. The setting must include things such as background music, dim lights, and illusion. The romance addict is forever searching for the feelings or settings that are often portrayed in popular music, movies, or novels. The dishonesty is perpetuated with a focus on the future rather than current reality. The addict is preoccupied with what kind of new romantic illusion can be created, rather than with being present with the person.

Denial. Because reality is not as exciting as fantasy, denial is important to the romance addict. The nonentertaining aspects of the real world are not allowed. Even though the addict has had numerous disappointments, he continues to believe the next encounter will fulfill his unquenched appetite. Denial includes maintaining a veil of vagueness and ambiguity. The addict does not make definite decisions or commitments to himself or to the other person.

Low self-esteem. The romance addict has a long history of failure. Her attempts at creating and maintaining the fantasy have consistently fizzled; her treasured illusions have never come about; but she hangs on to the belief that if only she were more perfect, her true lover would overcome her with passion and attention. Constant reading of romance novels, viewing the TV soaps, and buying lacy underwear or exotic perfumes helps perpetuate the myth, but does nothing to create a new reality.

Superficial appearance. Romance addicts do not really want to know their partners. They want to look good with them. The male wants a beautiful woman, and the female addict wants a tall, handsome stranger on her arm. The key is that the mate remain a stranger. There is no goal of intimacy, sharing, or long-lasting friendship. The setting and the people in the setting must look good and have an element of mystique. Commitment, understanding, and sharing are not part of the package. Because the focus is on the fix, the addict often misses the experience itself. He is so busy saying, "Look at me. I'm swimming naked under a waterfall with a beautiful woman," that he misses the experience. The illusion of the experience is more important than the experience itself. Then, of course, it is important to talk about these experiences. In fact, talking about them is as important as having them. The other person is only a stage prop that completes the fantasy experience.[2]

Instant intimacy. "Our eyes met from across the room and there was a magnetism that drew us unexplainably together." "I saw her in that red dress and fell instantly in love." Romance addicts are experts in what they call instant intimacy. In reality, they seek instant gratification. They are terrified of real closeness, and use their addictive behavior to avoid it.

Mood alteration. The romance addict can get high from a daydream, a song, a scene, a romantic memory, or a cause. Everywhere he turns in our society, there is a source for the fix. Media, movies, TV, and advertisements can all be sources for a mood-altering experience. The problem, as with any addiction, is that the fix is never enough. It doesn't last and is never as satisfying as the fantasy.

The chemistry of romance. Research in the past ten years has shown there is even a chemical side to romance addiction. According to Michael Liebowitz, author of *The Chemistry of Love,* a substance known as phenylethylamine or PEA is released in the brain when we fall in love. The PEA molecule, which is considered an excitatory amine, bears striking structural similarity to the pharmaceutically manufactured stimulant amphetamine. Liebowitz regards the accelerated use of PEA, which occurs during infatuation, as the key to feelings of excitation, exhilaration, and euphoria. The language of love is poetry. The language of the brain where love abides is chemistry.[3][4]

There is a remarkable biological parallel between pathological drug use and the unhealthy need for affection. Becoming dependent on romance can be described as a dynamic process with two distinct biochemical phases: *infatuation* and *attachment.*

Infatuation is usually an experience of heightened energy and feelings of euphoria. The initial period of psychosexual attraction produces increased concentrations of the neurotransmitter-like substance phenylethylamine. The brain responds to this chemical in much the same fashion that it would to amphetamine or cocaine. Infatuated lovers seem to experience boundless energy, elation, and a remarkable sense of well-being. Those experiencing infatuation have no problem in "painting the town red" and then going to work, only to repeat the cycle day after day.

After a short time, however, the speedy feeling appears to reach a maximum level, and lovers begin to recognize that their relationship is on a plateau. The romance remains exciting, yet the remarkable sensations of invigoration and euphoria appear to be dwindling. In chemical terms, the pleasure of falling in love is derived from steady increases in the rate of PEA production. When the rate of PEA production begins to level off, the honeymoon is over.

At this point, one of several things might happen. The lovers may go into an amphetamine-like withdrawal. The ecstasy of the relationship is over and depression and pain of withdrawal takes over. The love addict may go on to another new, exciting, tantalizing infatuation relationship. Or the lovers may make the transition from zooming around in the fast lane to enjoying cuddles and a quiet evening at home. The latter is the *attachment* phase. The attachment phase is said to be an endorphin-mediated chemical relationship.

Endorphins and enkephalins are opiates produced by the body to control pain. Without them we would constantly suffer from the slightest injury. Not only do the endorphins and enkephalins reduce pain, but they also produce a euphoria much like that of opiates. Therefore, any substance that tends to reduce pain has a soothing effect on our emotions. Mood-calming activities also have the effect of releasing endorphins, which in turn decrease the number of neurotransmitter molecules released into the synapse. This, in turn, results in the feeling of well-being experienced during, and immediately following, these activities.

One well-known endorphin-releasing activity is eating

warm and pleasant-tasting food. It is the body's own endorphins that bring the relief from a sore throat upon eating warm soup. Another example is drinking warm milk. Ingesting warm milk releases endorphins which decrease the release of excitatory neurotransmitters. This results in a decreased rate of neurotransmission in the excitatory pathways, which soothes and calms the consumer. Warm milk also contains another ingredient that brings about a soothing effect on the central nervous system. This substance is the amino acid tryptophan, which enters the brain through the blood-brain barrier. Once inside the brain, tryptophan is converted to serotonin, which also decreases excitatory neurotransmission. This contributes to the overall relaxing effects of warm milk and helps the person to sleep.[5]

It is this same kind of endorphin-mediated chemical response that comes into play in the attachment phase of a romantic relationship. The initial feeling of intoxication, the giddy, breathless onrush of romantic excitement is replaced by a calm, relaxed state.

Apparently, there is a chemical contribution to relationship addiction, in both the infatuation and attachment phases. This helps explain the mood-altering characteristic of romance addiction. Let's return to the discussion of other characteristics.

Progressiveness. A cocaine addict eventually needs more and more drug to obtain a high. Romance addicts will spend increasing amounts of time in their reverie. They will remove themselves more and more from all aspects of their families, work, and relationships. It takes additional anticipation of romance to get the same fix. We just saw how chemistry plays a part in that process. Huge amounts of energy will be expended to try to sustain the feelings, but with decreasing effectiveness. Panic can set in as the addict tries to conjure up additional sources. This can lead to higher levels of risk, including illegal or dangerous activity.

Sex is often used as a vehicle for the romance addict, even when he has little interest in actual sex. The addiction is not maintained by the sexual experience, but by the anticipation of the procurement, ritual, or illusion surrounding sex. This progressive nature of addiction can result in the addict making unwise choices that expose him to disease, arrest, disclosure, embarrassment, violation of moral values, and physical danger.

One of my clients reported being in the waiting room of a massage parlor having signed up for the "special of the day." Already anxious, he nearly died of a heart attack, as from behind a newspaper he saw a highly respected member of his church leadership walk in and register for the same fix.

The problem is that even a traumatic experience of that type is soon overloaded by increased need, and the addict will take additional chances to get to his or her source.

Loss of morality. As the addict progressively loses control over the ability to stop or start her behavior, she moves away from truth and from compliance to her values and morals. Instead, she will engage in activities which are exclusively in service of her addiction. Broken relationships, wrecked homes and marriages, disease, dishonesty, and insensitivity to the needs and feelings of others become the norm. Christian values, once so important, are discarded as the addictive cycle progresses.

LEVELS OF ROMANCE ADDICTION[6]

There are four levels of romance addiction. Often, but not always, a person will progress from one level to another. The reason is that it takes more and more activity to sustain the level of excitement and anticipation that fuels the addictive need. Like levels in any type of addiction, these categories are not discreet. People can show behaviors on more than one level. While progressive, an addict at Level One is in just as much trouble as an addict at Level Four.

Level One. This level is primarily fantasy. The Level One addict usually does not act out his fantasy. However, much time is spent in reading romance novels, screening the TV guide for romantic programs, viewing romantic movies, and daydreaming about romantic adventures. The transition from activity to addiction comes when the fantasies become the primary focus of his life and the addict is powerless to control when he starts or stops the addictive behavior.

When romance fantasies begin to make a person's life unmanageable, that person has become a romance addict. An example is the mother who cannot attend to her children when her favorite "soap" is showing. As she avoids her feelings and relationships with others, reality recedes and fantasy takes over. She begins to exhibit the characteristics of addiction such as dishonesty, self-centeredness, and lack of control.

Level Two. Level Two addicts begin to act out their fantasies by having affairs, romantic encounters, and multiple marriages. Their behavior has a noticeable affect on others because they are spending more time and energy in creating the illusion. Reality testing shows some slippage. The person has greater and greater problems with control. He will start to pull away from those who are not instrumental in fulfilling his needs. If married, he becomes increasingly insensitive to the needs of his spouse and children. At this level, the romance addict is affecting the outside world in definite ways. His growing sense of unworthiness and low self-esteem becomes increasingly evident to those around him. His sense of right and wrong and personal integrity begins to go into a decline.

Level Three. All addictions are progressive. It takes more intensity to provide the fix. Level Three romance addicts actually need the thrill. They go to greater lengths to find their "sources." They begin to act out their addiction in such a way that it is harmful to themselves and others. It may even verge upon or include illegal behavior. They go into sexual situations that could be dangerous. It isn't the sex that motivates them but the romantic thrill. At this level, addicts will spend large sums of money to seek out romantic liaisons. They may go to faraway places and become involved with strangers, even putting themselves in danger, just to obtain the thrill. As personal and cultural values are ignored, moral deterioration is clearly evident. Families will be destroyed, children and spouses abandoned. For romance addicts, it really doesn't matter. They do what they have to do to get their fix. Involvement with married partners is continued even though it conflicts with the addict's personal ethics.

Violence may be precipitated to enhance the excitement. If this becomes a significant part of the illusion, we can say it moves to another level.

Level Four. This is violent romantic behavior. At this level the content of the romantic fantasies changes from candlelight and roses to knives and chains. The addict can get high only from violent, life-threatening situations. The ritual may include sex and another person. But it may also include taking personal risks that are seen by the addict as life-threatening and, therefore, romantic. Fantasies and movies are no longer enough. The romantic thrill may even be best accomplished alone. At this level, the addict may no longer make any pretense about having a relationship, but may seek out the thrill of being with someone who is really sick and potentially dangerous.

SELF-EVALUATION
To help you determine if you have a romance addiction, take the following test. Answer each of the questions as honestly as you can.

TEST FOR ROMANCE ADDICTION

_____ 1. Do you often think or fantasize about what or how it would be like to be in love?

_____ 2. Do you find yourself spending lots of time reading romantic novels or watching romantic TV programs or movies?

_____ 3. Do you expect that someday a truly fulfilling romantic encounter will take place in your life?

_____ 4. Have you ever felt out of control in regard to your interest or behavior in romantic things? You have tried to stop but couldn't.

_____ 5. Are you skilled in creating romantic, movielike, enchanting settings for you and your partner?

_____ 6. Is it difficult for you to make a real commitment to another person? You find yourself avoiding discussions that get too serious.

_____ 7. Do you struggle with a low self-esteem and often wish you could be someone else?

_____ 8. Do you enjoy being seen with a beautiful or handsome companion? How you look together is very important to you.

_____ 9. Has your experience included encounters where you instantly fell in love or knew you and your partner were meant for each other?

_____ 10. Do you often find yourself thinking about how you can recreate the good feelings associated with being in a romantic setting?

_____ 11. Is it difficult for you to share true and intimate feelings with another person?

_____ 12. Has your attraction to romance led you into situations that contradicted your personal values or standards, leaving you with feelings of guilt?

_____ 13. Have you found yourself needing to engage in increasingly intense or provocative situations or relationships in order to be satisfied?

_____ 14. Have you had to lie, deceive, or cover up some of your behavior so family or friends wouldn't find out what you were doing?

_____ 15. Has anyone said that you may be spending too much time, taking too many risks, or overdoing it a bit, in regard to your romantic interests?

How many times did you answer yes to one of the questions? If it was more than two or three, you need to consider the possibility you are addicted to romance. If you responded positively to more than five or six items, you are out of control and need to start your recovery immediately. Remember all addictions are progressive. You may not have gotten into trouble yet, but if things don't change, you eventually will hurt yourself and/or someone else.

WHAT TO DO?
You must begin with the recognition that you are hooked. This is the first step in understanding the basis of your addiction. Remember, you are still a valuable and important person. You have lost control of a portion of your life. Some things are out of balance. But you can get that control back and the balance restored. You are not bad or evil. God created you as His very own child to live in harmony. God wants that tranquility restored. Let's see how that process can begin.

There are five steps to recovery from romance addiction: awareness, decision, assessment, change, and maturity.

Awareness. The fact you are reading this section may mean you know you have an addictive relationship with romance. Awareness has two parts. The first is to know that there is such a thing as romance addiction. The previous description of characteristics, progression, and stages should have helped you to know the problem is real, powerful, and destructive. The second aspect of awareness is to know that you have a relationship with an experience or object that is addictive. This personalizes the awareness. It is no longer a "thing" out there that affects the general population. You are now able to admit you have a dependency problem and are out of control.

I will say it again and again: *Denial is the most common*

and damaging aspect of any addiction. When a person is trapped in the denial stage, there is no opportunity for recovery and change to occur. If you took the Romance Addiction Test honestly, and answered yes to more than three items, it is time to make a decision to regain control of your life.

Decision. If you assessed your life and found signs that you are infatuated with and dependent on romantic experiences to alter your mood, you now have to make a decision. You must decide whether to keep the status quo or to work toward recovery and change. It will not be easy — habits are hard to change. You have used romance to deaden the pain, avoid intimacy, and exercise some type of personal control. Romance and all of its attachments may have given you an illusion of gain or a feeling of greater self-esteem or security. Perhaps it gave you a sense of pleasure, comfort, and success. It may have helped you deal with fear, loneliness, or depression. Romantic involvement may have helped you avoid pain, or have given you a sense of control about when and how you alter your mood. These are called secondary gains. Think about what your attachment to romance has contributed to your life. You will need this list of gains in just a minute.

Change means learning a new way of doing things. Because you may have tried to stop before, you are pessimistic about your chances of regaining control. Your discouragement and depression tend to block this decision. Your feelings say, "It's no use. I'll never be in control." But it *is* possible to change! Others have done it and so can you. You can choose to use the power of God and your personal gifts to bring about a renewed life!

Traditions or rituals have an important place in our history. This is also true for our addiction. May I suggest the following comparison. First take any item you may have used in your romantic endeavors — a romance novel, a TV guide, a picture of the person who is your romance attachment, or an article of clothing. Place that object in front of you. Now repeat these words:

I, (your name), give to you, (the object of your attraction), the power to make me whole and complete. Without you I am nothing. I must have you to make my life complete. You are necessary to give me (list your secondary gains, needs, desires, and goals) and you satisfy my needs for security, pleasure, and power. I surrender my power to you. I will do whatever you command in exchange for your promise to make me whole. If anybody or anything tries to come between us, I will do everything possible to keep us connected.

How did that feel? Was it enabling and freeing? I now suggest you try the following ritual. This one is designed to help you regain control and start the process of recovery.

I, (your name), now reclaim the gift of God's power. I renounce the power of (the object of your attraction). I claim God's promise of a free and abundant life. I know I can obtain (list your needs, desires, and goals) through the grace of God and the power of discernment and self-control that He can give me. I will be free of the bond that has been created by my relinquishment of power to the illusion of romantic fantasies. No longer will I look to romance, and all of its promises, as being my greatest need. In the future, romance may be an important part of an intimate relationship. However, romantic experiences will come about by my developing feelings of love for another person and not out of fear or attempts to manipulate.

How did this ritual compare to the first one? How and why is it different? If you can participate in this ritual of freedom, you have enhanced and symbolized your *decision* to begin the journey.

Assessment. Once you have decided to renounce the control of romance addiction in your life, it is important to explore and assess the complex dynamics of your addiction. This is not an easy task, but it is crucial to discover the circumstances, beliefs, and experiences that lead to your addictive behavior.

As you undertake this, pray for strength and guidance. Remember your own powerlessness. Only God can give the ability to overcome addiction. The purpose of this step is to get some idea of the nature, scope, and inner workings of your attachment to romance. Ask God to help you with the process. It is much too monumental to go it on your own.

One of the best tools for self-assessment is a daily journal. Near the end of each day reflect back over the previous twelve hours or so. I would suggest three categories for you to consider in your entries — feelings, thoughts, and situations. Monitor your feelings through the course of the day. Do you feel fear, loneliness, depression, joy, anticipation, anger, etc.? It doesn't matter what the feeling is, just that you notice its existence. Then describe in your journal the beliefs, thoughts, or self-talk that accompanied each of the feelings. Perhaps you felt a little anxious and then thought about reading or watching TV to take your mind off of your anxiety. Maybe you even argued with yourself about whether this was a good idea. Try to describe that dialogue in your journal. Finally, make a note of the situation in which the feelings and thoughts took place. For example, you might recall that your car was in the shop so you couldn't get some errands done. You didn't feel like ironing or reading, so you were looking for something to erase the boredom. It was then you began to think about your lack of purpose or meaning in life, and began to feel anxious.

A journal accomplishes several purposes. Although I have suggested three components to your entries, sometimes you need to just express feelings. At those times, let the feelings flow. Don't try to interpret or understand. Just feel the feelings. Sometimes trying to make sense out of what's happening is premature. You may just need to write about your feelings for a number of days. Learning to express your feelings is a very important function of journaling.

In the context of assessment, the additional purpose of a journal is to look for pattern and themes. Over a period of several weeks you will begin to see repetitions of behavior. Your "acting out" in regard to romantic activity or content probably will fall into a pattern. Understanding this pattern will help you with reestablishing control.

Writing is good because you can review previously written material. For many people, writing also draws on more of the total learning experience and facilitates understanding that otherwise would not take place. However, if you are an auditory learner, dictating your journal entries into a tape recorder may be a good alternative. Then you can play back prior days' entries and perhaps make short notes about specific patterns.

Another very good idea is to work with a counselor who understands addictive behavior. As you recall earlier experiences and the connected feelings and thoughts, more of these patterns will emerge. This awareness and insight will help you make necessary changes.

Reading books, listening to tapes, attending seminars, or talking to friends or family are other common ways to expand understanding of your addiction. I have listed some useful resources in the appendix of this book for your consideration.

Change. Making a decision or trying to assess your addiction is part of change. Before, you denied the significance of your attraction to romance. Now you can acknowledge something is wrong. That represents change. What else can you do?

One of the most important changes is to join a support group. This can be a group specifically designed for those with romance addictions, or a general group with a more generic focus. Probably the more specific the better. Another excellent option would be a Twelve Step group. Modeled after Alcoholics Anonymous, there are an increasing array of Twelve Step programs for specific needs. Sex and Love Addicts Anonymous, Sexual Addicts Anonymous, and Sexaholics Anonymous are the best-known groups that would fit the needs of a romance addict. Look in your telephone directory for a local meeting, or refer to the appendix of this book for the national office of each of these organizations.

Before you commit to any program, take time to examine the values and procedures of the people involved in it. Quality control is always a problem for any organization. I cannot guarantee that every resource material mentioned here will match up to your unique needs and values. That is why a personal counselor or therapist can be so helpful in the recovery process.

The Twelve Step program has been adapted to the more specific Christian context. When the general reference to a *Higher Power* is changed to a specific and personal relationship with Jesus Christ and God the Father, the Twelve Steps can be extremely valuable. To this end I have devoted an entire chapter to the Twelve Steps showing how they can be a vital framework for your recovery. Also, the steps I have outlined in this section of awareness, decision, assessment, change, and maturity, closely parallel items in the

Twelve Steps. Therefore, some valuable suggestions that could be discussed here will be presented in the Twelve Step chapter. Be sure to pay particular attention to that material regardless of your area of attachment.

What about abstinence? During the recovery from romance addiction, it is necessary to maintain abstinence from the mood-altering experience or object. For the romance addict this means no movies, TV, reading material, or other triggers for the acting-out behavior. This also means no involvement in "romantic" relationships. Now is no time to try to form a deep, intimate relationship. Give yourself at least a year of recovery and sobriety, and probably two, before allowing yourself the opportunity.

Obviously, if you are married, there is a relationship to maintain. That relationship probably needs lots of help. Your addiction to romance has undoubtedly caused some distrust and hurt. Your spouse needs to attend an Al-Anon or codependent group and will also need to accompany you to counseling at some point, but probably not at the beginning. Romance addiction is an escape from intimacy. You will need help and time to learn how to handle intimate connections. This is a time to heal your insides. God must help you change from the inside out. This does not mean an existing relationship should end or be avoided, just that you need internal healing.

Friends are an important part of changing. Now is a time for friendship skills. You need to learn that intimate relationships are meant to be built on friendships first. Then, the progression from sharing, listening, and keeping confidences can move to romance and commitment. Friendship skills are different from the manipulation and control patterns learned in your addiction.

Learn to take care of yourself. Take control of your diet and exercise; practice good hygiene; and spend time in meditation, prayer, and Bible study. Try to manage your time so you are not terrorized by those things called "urgent." Addictions occur in clusters so that often several areas of life are out of control. You don't need an overly ambitious agenda. Take your time. "Small steps for little feet" is a good maxim here. Be moderate, even in your recovery. Now is not the time for crash diets or extreme changes in lifestyle. Take seriously the need to break your bond to romance, but be sensible as you go about it.

Finally, be prepared for old memories to arise. Addictions cover over old hurts. As you stop using mood-altering experiences to avoid the pain, much of that pain will surface and will seem to get worse before it gets better.

Betty called her friend from the support group in a panic. "I can't stand it one more minute. I've got to do something. I'm about to go out of my mind. I've been having terrible dreams about dark, scary creatures. I wake up in a cold sweat, and my pillow is covered with tears."

Betty went on to describe a volcano-like sensation. It was like an explosion of feelings was about to take place any minute. What was happening was a repressed memory of childhood sexual abuse which was about to come to her conscious awareness. Much of her previous addictive behavior was functioning to keep the pain of the childhood trauma from surfacing. Now, with her sobriety and recovery proceeding fairly well, those old memories were coming forward.

This is definitely a time when a professional therapist is necessary. You will need someone who can help you deal with the intense feelings and sort through all of the confusion. A support group for those with abusive histories may also be helpful. You need a safe place to feel your feelings, express your ideas, and receive support and encouragement.

Recovery is like repairing an old house. You think all the bathroom needs is new fixtures and a paint job. You take out the old bathtub and find the floor is rotted out. You remove the flooring and find the foundation is also in need of replacement. What appeared to be a simple weekend project takes a month. But it has to be done. You don't want to put in a new bathtub on top of a rotten floor. The same is true of overcoming an addiction. There are often surprises and it is hard work, but the final product is worth it!

Maturity. Romance addiction is one way to avoid intimacy and cover up pain. As our recovery takes place we must learn how to accept ourselves and, eventually, learn to accept others. We are instructed to love our neighbor and to love ourselves (Matthew 19:19). Intimacy will never happen until you can first love yourself.

The first step in self-love is understanding our fundamental nature. We each need to ask, "Who am I?" God has made us whole and complete (2 Corinthians 5:17; Colossians 3:10). We will grow to that essential completeness only if we are able to understand and accept ourselves as God sees us. It takes courage to accept a self with a history of addiction, pain, and poor choices. We have vivid evidence that our personhood contains defects and weaknesses, but we can still learn to accept ourselves. Our sense of being or knowing who we are starts with the admission of weakness. In this case, it is the presence of an addiction to romance.

The reason we can be brazen enough to tackle this question is founded on the fact of God's unconditional love for us (John 3:16; 16:27). We are loved regardless of our failures. We have done nothing to deserve God's love, yet it is freely given (Romans 3:24). God loves us in spite of our attachments or lack of control.

These are the facts of our value and importance to God. The next step is to accept the love of God. For the addict this is hard. All we have to do is simply receive His gift which is freely given.

Another part of the maturing process is having a sense of purpose. While the addictive personality was being formed, the preoccupation was on the need to avoid pain or alter our mood by participating in a certain experience. Over time nothing else mattered. In recovery, something else must begin to matter. The addict must begin to address the issue of our purpose for living. The question is, "Why am I here?"

A sense of purpose gives direction for life, and this direction is crucial. If we don't know where we are going, we may well get lost. Knowing our purpose under God gives us a compass bearing.

Our calling is to be God's representatives on earth. As stewards of all that He created, we have the major purpose of bearing fruit (John 15:16). As we use our abilities and gifts in service to others, the fruits of love, joy, peace, patience, kindness, goodness, faithfulness, gentleness, and self-control will be planted, nourished, and multiplied (Galatians 5:22-23).

To bear fruit, then, becomes our response to the nagging question, "Why do we exist?" We can know that God placed us here. Living a life of faith can give us a solid sense of purpose. As we focus on the maturation process, knowing our labors are to result in love, joy, peace, etc., we will be better able to keep on course and fulfill our destiny.[7] If we learn to accept ourselves, we then can think about forming an intimate attachment with another human being. As we have the vertical relationship right with God, our horizontal relationships with other humans can more readily take place in a healthy, mature manner.

N O T E S

1. Portions of this section adapted from Anne Wilson Schaef, *Escape from Intimacy* (New York: Harper & Row), 1989, 47–50.
2. *Ibid.,* 56.
3. Michael Liebowitz, *The Chemistry of Love* (Boston: Little-Brown), 1983.
4. Ron Rosenbaum, "The Chemistry of Love," *Esquire,* June 1984, 100–111.
5. Harvey Milkman and Stanley Sunderwirth, *Craving for Ecstasy: The Consciousness & Chemistry of Escape* (Lexington, Massachusetts: D.C. Heath), 1987, 49.
6. Adapted from Schaef, *Escape from Intimacy,* 51–52, 62–66.
7. Grant Martin, *Transformed by Thorns* (Wheaton, Illinois: Victor Books), 1985, 74–86.

CHAPTER THREE

RELATIONSHIP ADDICTION

Do You Need to Have Another Person?

● Wayne and Rose had been dating for six months. The courtship had seemed like a roller-coaster ride with all of its ups and downs. One day Rose would feel like the most cherished queen of the land. But following one of their frequent fights, she didn't think she could stand to be around Wayne for another minute.

Rose had tried to break off the relationship on three or four occasions. But each time, Wayne would apologize for being so cruel, promise never to act that way again, and Rose would decide to try it again.

She couldn't figure out what was happening. There was something about being with Wayne that she couldn't do without. It was like she needed to be with him sometimes, or else she would get depressed and anxious. Rose figured that meant she really did love him after all and should continue to see him.

This chapter is about being hooked on relationships. In such relationships the addictive element is a compelling need to bond and remain bonded with a particular person, or at least to maintain an illusion or fantasy of a relationship.

Underlying relationship addiction is a sense of incompleteness, emptiness, despair, or hurt. Further, the relationship addict believes this pain can be remedied only through his connection to someone outside himself. This someone then becomes the center of his existence, and he is willing to do great personal damage just to be able to keep the connection intact.

TYPES OF RELATIONSHIP ADDICTIONS

There are two types of relationship addictions. In Type I the person is addicted to the *possibility* of having a relationship. This can be any relationship, real or imagined. In Type II, the person is addicted to a specific relationship with a particular person. Commitment, or somehow nailing down the relationship, becomes the absolute priority. Then comes the task of hanging on to it for dear life, in spite of any danger signs to the contrary.

In the first type, the individual is hooked on the *idea* of a relationship, and in the second type the addict is hooked on the *person.*[1]

Type I relationship addicts are hooked on the concept of a relationship. They focus on the illusion of a relationship and ignore the reality of the actual person. The fantasy or belief that they have a relationship is the mood-altering drug. The obsession is with a supposed relationship, not with a real person. Type I addicts are obsessed with having a relationship, any relationship. And when they have relationships, they have them addictively. They exhibit the same kind of frantic acquisitiveness as a drunk hunting for a drink. Any fix will do. They are always scanning their world for possibilities.[2]

Type II relationship addicts are somewhat more selective. They attach themselves to a person and must have that person. They are willing to sacrifice their personal values and sense of integrity to hold on to the person. This is done even though emotional and physical abuse is present.

PATTERNS OF RELATIONSHIP ADDICTION

Using Carne's addiction cycle (which we will discuss in chapter 4), Anne Wilson Schaef describes both types of relationship addicts as showing the following pattern.

Preoccupation means that the person has an obsession with a relationship. This state of being has a trancelike, mood-altering effect. There is a total absorption with the relationship. Routine tasks are omitted, and responsibilities for work, school, or family are left undone in order to dwell on the obtaining or maintaining of the relationship.

Ritualization is the next part of the cycle. The addict must engage in behaviors that relate to establishing a relationship. This includes losing weight, and changing hairstyles, clothes, or makeup. Ritualized courting behavior such as going to specific gathering places like bars, dating clubs, or church socials may also take place.

Compulsive relationship behavior, equivalent to the drinking phase of the alcoholic, now takes place. The addict must establish a relationship as soon as possible. Discussing marriage, getting engaged or married, obtaining a commitment, or somehow securing down the relationship becomes the absolute priority. Then comes the task of hanging on to it for dear life, in spite of any conflicting danger signs.

Despair is the final stage in the addictive cycle for both types of relationship addicts. The fix is not working. The illusion is not taking place. Reality does not come close to matching the fantasy, but they feel hopeless and powerless to do anything about it.[3]

CHARACTERISTICS OF RELATIONSHIP ADDICTION

Blindness. Relationship addicts, particularly Type I, need a relationship. They care little for what the other person is like. They just need to have someone. They are blind to their need for understanding and compatibility. They do not compare to see if backgrounds, values, or goals match. They either need to be needed, or are so needy that they charge ahead oblivious to their ignorance.

Deceptiveness. Both types usually have developed interpersonal skills such as listening, sharing superficial feelings, and apparent empathy, to a very effective degree. Relationship addicts have learned to become experts in the techniques of having a relationship. They appear to be open and genuine, but it is all a con. What appears to be behavior that creates intimacy turns out to be skill in manipulation and control. This type of addict is able to feign a relationship, but is not able to let his or her true feelings surface.

Terror of being alone. Relationship addicts can't stand to be alone. Their identity is bound up in having a relationship. They have no sense of being, mission, or purpose within themselves. If one relationship ends, they must get another one as soon as possible. Without learning anything from the mistakes of the past, relationship addicts take all of their unresolved issues into new liaisons.

Selective forgetting. Relationship addicts, especially those in Type II, have selective amnesia. In order to keep the relationship, they selectively avoid or deny the severe problems that happened last year, last month, or yesterday.

There is a tendency to make excuses or minimize events or characteristics which have caused pain. Relationship addicts will lie to themselves and others about any sacrifices they are making to keep the relationship alive. They may sacrifice the well-being of their children or themselves in order to sustain their fix. Often they will believe that suffering and loving are the same since they go together. If they are suffering they must be in love because it hurts so much. Conversely, if they are not suffering, they must not be in love.

Loss of integrity. Both types will compromise their values to maintain the illusion. In spite of moral or spiritual standards, addicts will do whatever seems necessary to keep the dream alive. They spend so much energy taking care of the other person, or cultivating the source, that they do not enhance their own spiritual or personal growth. As the addictive process becomes more entrenched, they are increasingly unable to comprehend their helplessness or too exhausted to do anything about their own needs.

Control. Relationship addicts believe they can make relationships happen by their own determination. They hold on to the myth that they can make another person love them through sheer persistence. As a result the addict becomes progressively more controlling, defensive, and blaming.

Loss of personal identity. Male relationship addicts believe they cannot live without a wife, and women believe they have no identity without a husband. Single persons believe they must have partners. The belief of all relationship addicts is that they must be part of a couple. The relationship addict is looking to the relationship to identify who he or she is. There is no concept of establishing an identity of their own outside of a partnership. The misbelief is, "Having you is the greatest need of my life. Therefore, if I don't have you, there is no reason for me to exist."

Anxiety and depression. Since the addict has made the relationship the source of her validity, meaning, and security, she must hold on to it. This is asking the relationship to meet all of one's needs, which is impossible. The addict, at some level, is aware of this dilemma, and strives harder to control the situation. But because she cannot control the other person or make him love her, the addict becomes more desperate. This leads to more dramatic encounters, including accusations and fights. These episodes create more feelings of insecurity and lead to feelings of anxiety and depression.

Dependency. Relationship addicts will cling to a relationship even when they know it is destructive. They are caught in a crazy dilemma. They recognize the situation is unhealthy, but they can't do anything to change it. They can't trust themselves to distinguish the difference between good and bad decisions.

Issues of submission and headship. Many women in the church have been taught that the secret to a happy marriage is to accept a dependent role. The recipe calls for the submissive wife to adapt to the husband regardless of the cost to her own personhood. Many well-intentioned wives have lived in a codependent relationship which feeds both their need to be needed and the husbands' need to be pampered. I have written about how the misuse of headship and submission has contributed to abuse in my two books *Please Don't Hurt Me* (Victor Books) and *Counseling for Family Violence and Abuse* (Word Books).

God does not intend for the woman to be a doormat or slave to her husband, nor is the husband to be a dictator or selfish child. This is where the concept of mutual submission comes in. God's order for marriage does not foster relationship attachment or codependency. In Ephesians 5:21-33, Paul begins with the explicit statement, "Submit to one another out of reverence for Christ." Paul is teaching that marital relationships are to be reciprocal and accountable. There must be equal responsibility for growth. Partners have the shared responsibility to look after the needs of the spouse as well as their own.

Mutual submission means both the partners will adapt. The husband sometimes does what his wife needs, even if it conflicts with his own desires. The wife is responsible to do the same, but not all of the time.

The goal of marriage is oneness (Genesis 2:24). With this goal in mind, Paul instructs the couple to develop a mutual relationship, in which each person attempts to love Christ and develop a servant's heart (Ephesians 5). The emphasis is not on one person's domination or another person's submission, but on self-giving servanthood. Paul's description of Christ's self-sacrificing action on behalf of the church is intended to portray the marital relationship as possessing the qualities of responsibility and initiative—the responsibility to act in love and initiative to act in service.

In the final analysis, there is nothing addictive about

God's design for marriage. The principle of mutual submission is an open and creative opportunity. The key ingredient here is choice. There are a variety of options for conducting a marriage. A couple has the freedom to grow. To be submissive means to yield in humble and intelligent obedience to an authority that God has ordained. This is done out of freedom and love, not out of addictive compulsion or fear. Both persons are free to choose the pattern that best fits them. Dependency, on the other hand, has no choice to it, and the outcome is bondage.[4]

LEVELS OF RELATIONSHIP ADDICTION

Level One. Schaef calls this level *anorexic* relationship addiction. Persons at this level are obsessed with avoiding relationships. This level includes those who are obsessed with relationships, yet do everything to avoid them. Such persons can appear phobic and frightened. They believe they should be part of a couple but deep down are terrified of that ever happening. As these addicts progress further into their obsession, they become more and more isolated. Because of that isolation, they may never be detected as addicts or might use any number of other addictions to cover up this core addiction.[5]

Level Two. This addict spends much of her time in fantasied relationships. These fantasies differ from romantic or sexual fantasies in that the focus is rarely on moonlight and roses. The fantasy is on being coupled with another person. Schaef reports there is little content to the fantasy of a Level Two addict other than the coupledness or the need for the belief that hers is a real relationship. She can have a fantasy relationship with someone she does not even know, and that person can be completely unaware of it. The point of addiction occurs when the addict begins to believe in the reality of these fantasies and mold her life around the illusions. The fantasies begin to interfere with work, friends, and family. She gets an addictive high from the fantasy relationship, and becomes confused and withdrawn.

Level Three. On this level are the people who are acting out their addictive behavior in relationships. Often addicts at this level have been in many relationships, going from one to the next. Some may stick with one even though it is not satisfying, since the important thing is to be in a relationship. When things go sour, there is another person waiting in the wings to call onstage. Addicts at this level marry people they do not even know or like, just to be married. There is a frantic quality to their quest for relationship; terror is present if they think they may be alone. People will endure abuse and put up with painful, destructive partnerships just to have the emotional fix of a relationship. Both men and women can display this form of addiction.

Level Four. Addictive relationships can be physically, mentally, and spiritually fatal. The process seems to grind the addicts down. Chronic pain, migraine headaches, and other physical symptoms can result. At this level addicts have lost contact with any awareness that they have options and so they stay in physically dangerous situations. Their judgment is so impaired and self-esteem is so low that they cannot mobilize themselves and are frequently suicidal. The threat of being without the relationship object evokes violence of one kind or another. Chemical abuse frequently occurs at this level. The relationship addiction has reached a level where nothing matters.[6]

SELF-EVALUATION
Now, let's take this information and apply it to your situation. Below is a checklist containing the general features of relationship addiction. Read through these characteristics. If your relationship meets three or more of the criteria listed below, then an addiction may be present. Take the results seriously. The hardest part of dealing with an addiction is to admit that you have one. Try not to minimize or explain away the symptoms if they are present. If you doubt your present ability to view the situation objectively, seek out a friend or counselor who can help you see more clearly. Here are the signs.

SIGNS OF RELATIONSHIP ADDICTION

    1. The first indication that you are experiencing an addiction is *compulsiveness*. Nonaddictive love involves being able to freely choose another person. One of the key signs of an addiction is that you are not able to control when you stop or start an activity. One of the consequences of this compulsive drive is a loss of freedom. Your thinking then becomes, "I must remain with this person even if the relationship is bad for me." The result is that you feel powerless to control your feelings or behavior with regard to your lover.

Those who become addicted usually lack confidence in their ability to cope without some form of support, real or imagined, from a love object. This chronic and intense form of lovesickness, sometimes called hysteroid dysphoria, is characterized by depression, depletion of energy, and increased appetite in response to feeling of rejection. On the other hand, when a romantic figure shows only a minimal sign of approval, the lovesick person reacts with increased energy and euphoria out of proportion to the situation at hand.

If you've broken up (seriously) at least twice, yet you always make up, you need to take a look at the relationship.

____ 2. The second indication that a relationship is addictive is the presence of anxiety or *panic*. These feelings arise at the thought of not being able to have access to your lover. Alcohol or substance abusers will feel panic when they are not sure where they will find their next drink. People in an addictive relationship will likewise experience overwhelming panic at the thought of breaking the relationship. An example would be a college coed sitting down to write her boyfriend a letter ending the relationship, but after countless attempts and consuming a whole box of stationery, her anxiety becomes so great she decides "she just can't do this to him."

____ 3. A third sign of addiction is the high need for *immediacy*. You require frequent emergency "pow-wows" with your lover. Whether at work, school, or social settings, you find yourself making panic phone calls, skipping appointments, avoiding responsibilities, or otherwise feeling driven to make immediate contact with your lover. You have to see or talk to him/her right now. And this pattern occurs often.

____ 4. A fourth symptom of an addictive relationship is the *progression* of a downward spiral. There are more disagreements, fights, misunderstandings, and unhappiness. You may feel you're doing everything possible to keep things in balance, but it just isn't working. Interest wanes, thoughts about other relationships or options more frequently come to mind. Finally, more and more of the following danger signs are present.

DANGER SIGNS IN A RELATIONSHIP

____ a. **Verbal put-downs.** Supermacho, caustic, sarcastic humor directed at partner, strong opposition to equality of male and female. Failure to listen to your feelings and needs, or share his or her own feelings with any kind of depth.

____ b. **Uncontrolled anger.** Sudden flare-ups, major disagreements over minor issues. Avoidance of resolution. Refusal to compromise. Frequent fights followed by remorse and making up, only to have the same cycle repeat. Driving habits can be very revealing—high risk maneuvers, horn honking, verbal or physical threats, speeding, intense body language, severe braking and acceleration.

_____ c. **Physical abuse.** Any type of hitting, threats, or aggressive gestures directed toward you or anybody else.

_____ d. **Disrespect toward parents.** Particularly a female toward her father and a male toward his mother. Is there history of abuse? Likelihood of being an abuser is quite high if the person has been abused. Highly critical parents can leave scars.

_____ e. **Chronic lateness.** If consistently and persistently late, there is a reason. May be rebellion, passive anger, pure arrogance—a way of showing that his/her needs are more important than yours. Can even be result of hidden hostility—may get a kick out of seeing you wait.

_____ f. **Irresponsible behavior.** Lack of reliability, doesn't keep promises. How does he treat other friends? You may seem to be an exception during courting phase, but it probably won't last. Problems with loyalty, two-facedness, failure to keep confidences. Do you hear others report things your partner has said or done that you don't want to believe? Is he/she very disorganized, a poor manager of time, an undisciplined little child? Tendency is to think you can rescue and change him/her into someone else. Don't. It won't happen.

_____ g. **Selfishness.** Self-serving behavior. Eating and buying habits. How do they spend their money? Any evidence of ability to give to others without any strings attached?

_____ h. **Jealousy.** Lots of questions about your use of time, demanding accountability of everything you do. Frequent phone calls questioning your whereabouts. Reluctance to allow you to spend some time with friends.

_____ i. **High dependence.** Strong need to either be needed, or to be taken care of. Low self-esteem. Makes statements about inability to survive without you. Unable to make decisions apart from your assistance, accompanied by anger and blame if you don't help, or if your advice doesn't work out.

_____ 5. The fifth sign of an addiction is symptoms of _withdrawal._ A person who finally ends an addictive relationship may suffer agony like that of a substance abuser who goes cold turkey. There may be physical pain, crying, sleep disturbances, anxiety, depression, and belief that there is no way to stop the pain except by going back to the relationship. This craving can become so great as to defeat the very best of intentions and drive you right back into the clutches of the addiction.

_____ 6. The sixth indication of an addictive relationship is that if, and when, the relationship is really over (or you think about it being over) you feel the lostness, aloneness, and _emptiness_ of a person eternally exiled. But after the mourning period, there is a sense of _liberation_, triumph, and accomplishment. In a non-addictive loss, there is a slow, sad acceptance and gradual healing.

———— 7. The final and important sign of addiction is *denial.* Your friends and family say you're in a bad relationship, but you don't agree. Even though your objective judgment, and even the opinion of others, tells you the relationship is bad for you and it probably won't get any better, you take no effective steps to break away. Furthermore, you give yourself reasons for staying in the relationship that aren't enough to balance out the negatives in the relationship.

How did you do? If you had three or more of the general characteristics and three or more of the danger signs, you may well need to make some changes.

WHAT TO DO?

Your recovery starts by coming to the awareness that you are attached to a relationship in an unhealthy way. Then you must see how your addiction works and become free enough of it so you can decide whether to work to improve the relationship, accept it as it is, or leave it and live with the consequences of your decision. For the married person the option of leaving may not be available, so the focus has to be on how to change the destructive nature of the relationship. If you or your spouse is abusive, you may want to read my book *Please Don't Hurt Me* (Victor), for suggestions on how to deal with your situation.

If you see by reading this chapter that you may be a relationship addict or a codependent person, the following suggestions will help you work on your own personality. This can be done along with marriage counseling to help move the marriage into a more balanced union. Having a firm commitment to marriage and working very hard to stand for the marriage and make things work, is not addiction. Keep in mind the distinction between addiction and nonaddiction given in chapter 1. The difference between commitment and addiction can be very confusing, but they are not the same. The material given here is intended to help you achieve some clarity. You can then take your awareness and work toward a healthier marriage.

The following steps toward recovery are easy to list but very difficult to follow. Each step is important. Do not leave anything out.[7]

Get help. This first step includes everything from reading a book to making an appointment with a counselor. It may mean talking to your pastor about your situation or calling a community hotline for a list of resources. Getting help may include joining a support group or visiting a program that deals with incest, alcoholism, or spouse abuse. You may take an adult education class on stress or anger management. There are lots of things you might do. The idea here is that you decide to reach out.

Do not threaten your partner with your intentions. This may come across as blackmail or manipulation. You are doing this for yourself. But at the same time, you are acknowledging you can't handle this alone. You must face the reality that things have gotten worse, that no improvement is in sight, and that you are out of control.

The typical pattern is to consider reaching out for help during a crisis. You make a phone call, schedule an appointment, but somehow endure the crisis so that next week when you are scheduled to talk to the social worker it doesn't seem quite so bad. So you cancel the appointment because you're too busy or can't afford it. Don't get trapped into this pattern. Don't settle for a cycle of relief followed by the next inevitable crisis.

A common fear of those caught in an unhealthy relationship is that if you go for help, things will get worse, your partner will get angry, or the relationship will end. Particularly for those with a Christian or traditional view of marriage, this can be a major concern. Getting help does not mean the relationship will end, but that it most certainly needs to change. The last thing you need is for things to stay the same. Because addiction is progressive, things are likely to get worse. Staying the same is seldom an option.

Determine that you will recover, no matter what. There are two parts to this step. One is that there are no excuses. You cannot blame the other person or your disadvantaged childhood, God, or lack of money. You have the sole responsibility (with God's help) to learn to do things differently. Sure, it will be hard because there are many obstacles to overcome. But excuses don't cut it. If the addiction to the mood-altering experience of relationship attachment is going to be overcome, you are the one responsible to make it happen.

Addiction, by definition, means you are out of control. You are powerless over your addiction. Your life is unmanageable. The paradox of recovery is that in the middle of admitting your weakness, you must still make a choice to change. You are giving up. You must surrender to the truth of your addiction. At the same time you are making a rational decision to quit trying to do what you haven't been able to do—maintain control of your life. This act of admitting your powerlessness gives you the power to change your life. When you quit trying to battle the impossible, you are enabled to do the possible.

The second part of this step is to turn away from a focus on changing anybody else. No amount of energy, no magic formula, will bring about significant changes in another person. If you take the same energy and apply it to yourself, great things can happen! It is possible you have never before esteemed yourself as important or worthy. You now need to acknowledge your lack of control and power, but still affirm your worthiness. This is a difficult balance which will take some time to achieve. But as you reach out for help, attend meetings, write in your journal, talk to friends, and participate in other recovery activities, the ability to affirm yourself will come. Your release from the bondage of addiction must be a priority.

This commitment to your recovery demands a great deal of time and even money. It may be uncomfortable to carry through on these expenditures of resources. It can also feel wasteful. But think for a minute about what your acting out has cost you. How much was spent on objects, substances, or experiences to try to deaden the pain up till now? How about food, alcohol, cigarettes, loss of work, books, movies, or trips to help you escape? Think of the long distance phone calls made in times of crisis, of medical bills arising out of too much stress. If you honestly think about what your relationship addiction has cost you thus far, your total will probably be enormous. The investment in your health is bound to be more profitable.

Another important aspect of determining to recover is to anticipate withdrawal symptoms. If you decide to give up your addictive attachment either by ending a relationship or by changing how you relate, you are bound to experience depression, loss of sleep, altered eating patterns, or feelings of aloneness and emptiness. When these happen, it means you are doing something right, one of the hardest things you have ever done.

Join a support group. If you have been in a relationship with an alcoholic or substance abuser, find an Al-Anon group. If you are the child of an alcoholic, go to an Adult Child of Alcoholic (ACOA) support group. If you were abused as a child, find a Sons or Daughters United or other such group for adults who were abused as children. If you have been battered by your partner, contact services for battered women (or men) in your area. If you have abused alcohol or drugs, a Twelve Step AA group is suggested.

There may also be groups for romance, sexual, or relationship addictions which, of course, would be ideal. More and more churches are sponsoring recovery groups for specific needs. If your church doesn't have one, check around your community. Contact the local Christian counseling services. They will probably have several different groups available. If all else fails, start your own. Some of the books mentioned in chapter 9 contain instructions for conducting a group.

A support group is not just a place to swap horror stories. There should be encouragement, instruction, planning, acceptance, and hope. A support group is not a therapy group; don't expect this one resource to shoulder all of your recovery. A group does ask for a commitment. Some last for a fixed period such as twelve weeks; others are more open-ended. In the beginning, give it four to six sessions to see if the content and people fit your needs. Each group, regardless of its type, has unique characteristics and feel. Be willing to shop around a little to find one that fits. You would do at least this much for a pair of shoes.

Regular attendance is necessary to develop an adequate measure of trust. Or, if trust is difficult to come by, it is even helpful to try to express your lack of trust. You'll find most everybody else has, or has had, the same reluctance.

What else will you gain from a support group? As others share their stories, you will begin to identify with them and eventually be more in touch with your own self. As you see the inadequacies and shortcomings in others, you will be able to accept those same flaws in yourself. This will contribute to the development of your own self-acceptance, a crucial element in your recovery. As you eventually share out of your own experience, you will become less secretive and afraid. The group's acceptance of what has been so repulsive to you will allow your self-acceptance to grow.[8]

Another benefit is in the ideas and suggestions offered by the group. You will see and hear about different options for dealing with problems. You can learn from the successes and failures of others. You will also be able to laugh. In the middle of all of the pain, humor over the inevitable foibles of the group will contribute to your healing.

Joining a group allows the secret to be told. Your attendance reflects your acknowledgment of your addiction, trauma, or life circumstance. Letting a few people know about your struggle helps pave the way out of your isolation and bondage.

Develop a supportive network. Overcoming a long-standing relationship addiction arouses feelings so basic, so frightening and painful, that they can paralyze your will and cause you to cling compulsively to the very relationship you are trying to break. At this time your friends and/or family can serve as an auxiliary life-support system. It is good to have several people to call upon. One reason for having a network is that no one person can handle the weight for all of your neediness. Second, you will have more than one opinion given about how you are doing. This variety is mostly helpful. Third, each friend has different gifts or strengths to bear upon your needs. One may be a good listener who just lets you rant and rave. Another friend may be quite empathetic and hurt along with you when you need that. Some friends will be good for comic relief, others can give an objective, rational perspective. All together, these different friends will provide you a network of handholders, cheerleaders, tear-catchers, and ego-builders to help you along the journey of recovery.

Forming such a network requires trust. It might even be argued that if you had been able to form deep friendships, this whole compulsive attachment might not have developed. If you haven't been able to trust, perhaps you can use the urgency of this crisis in your life to help motivate you to take some risks. The support group mentioned earlier may be an excellent place to form some friendship bonds, if you have few others.

As you make or deepen friendships, pay attention to your thoughts and feelings about being close to people. Your fear may be based on beliefs such as: "Nobody cares about me." "Everyone is out for himself." "I have nothing to offer a friendship." "People will always reject me." "People will eventually hurt me." You probably had some real experiences which taught you these beliefs. But they are not always true. If you operate as if these statements are always true, your addiction will be harder to break. No one wants to enter a world of strangers who are likely to harm or hurt. Learning there are friends you can trust will contribute greatly to your recovery.

For further reading on building friendships, I would recommend *The Friendship Factor*, by Alan McGinnis, and *Intimate Connections* by David Burns. Both books contain more detailed steps for making close friends.

Continue your spiritual journey on a daily basis. Recovery from any addiction, including attachment to another person, requires a personal commitment to seek God's presence in your life. Relief from pains of the past is accomplished on a daily basis. A daily discipline of prayer and meditation is a vital component in recovery. In the past your addictive patterns caused you to worship false gods such as sex, romance, or idealized relationships. Now you must submit to continually seeking God's will and His presence in overcoming your addiction.

Spiritual growth occurs slowly and only through persistent effort. The components of both prayer and meditation must be a part of this discipline.

Authentic prayer often begins with a cry for help. For the recovering addict, this is perfectly appropriate. Keith Miller has written, "When I realize I am powerless—and that I am not God at all—and then come in contact with One who is God, 'Help!' may be the only sane prayer."[9]

Your prayers do not need to be wordy or complex. A simple statement of adoration for God, followed by statements of confession, need, and thankfulness, is sufficient. The model of the Lord's Prayer is perfect (Matthew 6:9-13;Luke 11:2-4). A simple pattern is to ask God for help in the morning to know and do His will for that day. At night, thank Him for getting you through another day and for whatever lessons you have learned. Something that simple can be effective.

A major motivation of your prayer is to follow Jesus' purpose as He sought His Father's will—"Your will be done, on earth as it is in heaven" (Matthew 6:10). For only God can bring about the miracle of a transformed life. Praying for the knowledge of God's will and the power to carry it out helps you set aside selfish motives. Through prayer you can receive reassurance of God's presence and know that He wants you restored to health.

You may have called out to God in times of crises and wondered if He would ever answer. All of us have had the feeling of being abandoned and ignored. Biblical heroes such as Jeremiah and David expressed the same feelings. But God has made some rather remarkable promises, and He does not lie. Here are a few of those promises:

- God will answer our prayers (Mark 11:24).
- God has never failed to keep His promises (1 Kings 8:56).
- God has guaranteed to be faithful (Deuteronomy 7:9; 1 Corinthians 1:9).
- He will deliver us from afflictions (Psalms 30:5; 41:3).
- He knows our limits (Isaiah 43:1-3; 1 Corinthians 10:13).
- He will comfort us in hard times (Isaiah 43:2).
- He will help remove obstacles (Luke 17:6).

That's quite a list! The choice is yours. You can continue trusting in your own understanding or learn to trust in the God who has never failed.

Prayer can be seen as our speaking to God. Meditation is an opportunity for God to speak to us. Both are necessary to complete the communication. Meditation is an important way of obtaining an understanding of God's will, setting aside our own agendas, and receiving what He has to show us. It is a time to be quiet. The old Quaker term is to center in. It allows the Holy Spirit to speak in that still small voice. The result is a quieting of our spirit. Meditation can help us calm down and relax. Time in meditation also allows us to become better acquainted with God. We are instructed that one of the conditions of bearing fruit is to hunger and thirst after righteousness (Matthew 5:6; 1 Peter 2:2). Meditation is a way of coming to know the truths of God, for it is that truth which can set us free.

More details about prayer and meditation will be given in chapter 9 as we discuss the Twelve Steps. Another excellent resource is Richard Foster's book *Celebration of Discipline*, which has chapters on both prayer and meditation for the Christian who is serious about spiritual growth. *Letting God: Christian Meditations for Recovering Persons* by A. Philip Parham is a good resource. This book provides one year of daily Scripture readings, meditations, and prayers for Christians in recovery.

Another aspect of your spiritual journey is to read something enriching each day. If you want to change your unconscious habits and hunger attachments, it will be important to read about God as well as pray to Him. The Bible is the best place to read about God. There you can discover the way God's will works out in the lives of people who live in the midst of problems and joys.

The Bible assumes God actually participates in the daily events of the world, both historically and presently. It contains a running account of His people's rebellion and battle with sin. Although we are children of God, He is continually trying to win us over, so that in our freedom we will choose to participate in the grand design of life that He envisions for us. The most important written information about God's nature and the development of our new life can be found in the Holy Scripture. This amazing Book contains profound pictures of wholeness, freedom, courage, and love.[10]

A major component in the spiritual journey is to let go of your determination to make things happen your own way. It didn't work, so give it up. Letting go of self-will means becoming still and receptive and waiting for guidance from a source outside of yourself. Spirituality requires a willingness to believe in the God who is able to make a difference in your life. No longer will you shoulder the responsibility of fixing everything. You have taken the first step in getting to know yourself and to improve the quality of your relationships. May you now find the meaning of true love.

N O T E S

1. Anne Wilson Schaef, *Escape from Intimacy* (New York: Harper & Row), 1989, 75.
2. *Ibid.*, 75, 90.
3. *Ibid.*, 75–76.
4. Grant Martin, *Please Don't Hurt Me* (Wheaton, Illinois: Victor Books), 1987, 165–172.
5. Schaef, *Escape from Intimacy*, 80.
6. *Ibid.*, 82.
7. Robin Norwood, *Women Who Love Too Much* (New York: Pocket Books), 1985, 220–261.
8. *Ibid.*, 232.
9. Friends in Recovery, *The Twelve Steps for Christians* (San Diego: Recovery Publications), 1988, 106.
10. Keith Miller, *SIN: Overcoming the Ultimate Deadly Addiction,* (San Francisco: Harper & Row). 1987, 155, 160.

SEXUAL ADDICTION
Is Sex Your Most Important Need?

● Joe could no longer live with the lie. He spilled out the facts of years of secret betrayal and bondage to his stunned wife. There were confused memories of childhood sexual abuse and numerous adolescent sexual encounters. Joe's story progressed to describe habitual masturbation, infatuation with pornography, and sexual binges while on business trips. The moral, legal, emotional, or medical consequences didn't matter. Joe believed he had to have his fix.

Joe is one of perhaps ten million persons in this country who is a compulsive sexual addict. Joe had fallen into a dangerous and devastating progression of sexual fantasy and behavior in order to compensate for certain voids in his life. Sex, and all of its connections, had become his singular attempt to fill the void in his soul.

There are many variations to sexual addiction. Every day there are thousands of husbands whose self-gratifying appetites cause them to demand nightly sex from their wives, thus causing the women to hate both their husbands and sex. Sexual fantasies getting out of control and leading to sexual encounters with coworkers, neighbors, and fellow church members is a common story. Another example is illustrated by the twenty-seven-year-old single woman who told her counselor, "I don't want to have sex with every guy I date. But no matter how hard I try, I can't seem to help it."

A common component of alcoholism or substance abuse is that the person has a pathological relationship with a mood-altering chemical. The same is true for the sexual addict. The sexaholic substitutes a deviant relationship with sexual thoughts and behavior for a healthy relationship. In many ways, addiction derives its compelling force from a failure to achieve intimacy. The obsession with sex replaces human bonding and caring.

For the addict, preoccupation with sexual things becomes more important than family, friends, and work. This relationship progresses to where sex in some form is necessary to feel normal. But to feel normal is also to feel isolated, guilty, and powerless, since the mood-altering activity is destructive and unhealthy. The person becomes dependent on sex to cope with life. Sex becomes the only source of nurturing that is within the control of the addict. Obtaining the mood alteration becomes the primary focus of life to which everything else is sacrificed or compromised.

PURPOSES OF SEXUAL ADDICTION

Sexual addiction serves several purposes. One of these is to reduce anxiety. We might even call this *tranquilizer sex.* Suppose a young mother is worried and anxious about the deteriorating communication in her marriage. She has attempted to share her feelings with her husband, but he keeps her at arm's distance. Enjoying no human intimacy, the wife retreats to romance novels, sexual fantasy, and self-stimulation to reduce her anxiety level. For a little while she feels better. While she can't control or change her husband's communication pattern, she can alter her mood. Hence, the potential for an addictive progression is established.

Probably all forms of sex could qualify as *intoxication.* The change in mood is euphoria and intense pleasure. While fantasizing about sex and engaging in sexual acting out, the person is dizzy with delight. Sexual experiences can make one ecstatic, blissful, and elated. One can be intoxicated with the pleasant feeling that overwhelms the body and mind. There is a physiological reaction that accompanies sex, making a sexual high one of the most pleasant human experiences. This is the way God meant it to be. But if the rapture of sex is taken out of the context of love, commitment, and ongoing communication, it gains tremendous power. Out of proper context, it stands out in dramatic disparity to the rest of life.

Another purpose of sexual addiction is to alleviate stress or reduce fear. Because it is like turning on the hallway light for a frightened child at bedtime, we'll call this *night-light sex.* A number of my clients have reported the only way they can relax or get to sleep is by having sex. Many wives have told me they can tell when their husband is under stress by the increased demand for sex. The problem here is the exclusive use of sexual activity to manage stressors or fears. Rather than to resolve the conflict, improve efficiency, eliminate barriers, etc. the addict escapes to sex.

Sexual addicts can also engage in sexual behavior for feelings of power and well-being. If this were more in the direction of health, I might call this orange juice sex. But I don't want to degrade a perfectly good food. So I'm calling this *sledge-hammer sex.* This is the heavy-handed misuse of power. Much of the motivation for sexual abuse of all types is due to this factor. Sex is seen as a conquest. It can also be an expression of anger and rage for the addict. Because of prior hurts, the addict channels resentment and revenge into sexual behavior. In an effort to cover up an inadequate self-esteem, the addict looks to sexual activity to make him feel better. The resulting feelings of well-being are a combination of exercising power over another person and a short-lived afterglow. It is not an expression of love and affection.

Excessive sexual behavior can also be used to avoid true feelings. This is *anesthesia sex.* Just as substance or alcohol are used to blot out pain, sexual attachments can be used to deaden feelings such as guilt, grief, or loss. Because sex has God-given positive qualities, it can be much more attractive than working through one's grief over the death of a parent, for example. Any and all feelings can be avoided by sexual acting out, but it is usually going to be the aftereffects of past traumas that will get the most attention.

Avoidance of intimacy applies to sexual addiction as well as all other forms of compulsions. An uncontrollable desire for a sexual high is truly an intimacy disorder. We'll call this *porcupine sex.* You don't want to get too close to a porcupine. Unless you're another porcupine, you're liable to get hurt. God ordained sex as a unifying and pleasurable component in marriage. First Corinthians 7:2-5, Genesis 2:24, Matthew 19:4-6, Mark 10: 7-9 tell us sex in marriage is approved by God and is intended for the pleasure of both husband and wife. Sex is intended to help bond a couple together in ways that are reciprocal and mutually satisfying. Sex is designed to be the highest form of intimacy. Addictive sex, however, has become a way to avoid intimacy. As such, sexual addiction is a spiritual, as well as emotional, break-down. The addict gradually moves away from the Master's plan for human relationships. Instead, the addict heads toward emotional and spiritual blindness.

CHARACTERISTICS OF SEXUAL ADDICTION

Many sex addicts come from dysfunctional families. Often this included *confusion* about family roles, expectations, and boundaries. The developing child was uncertain about how to please his or her parents. Blurred definition about mother/father or male/female roles existed, so the child was not able to model healthy adult behavior.

The issue of *boundaries* is very important. Many sex addicts have not learned how to set personal limits because appropriate limits were not present in their family of origin. For example, the child may not have had the privacy of his own room, or been allowed to require other people to knock before entering. Reading diaries or personal mail without reason, or violations of personal space, are other examples. Sexual abuse would be an obvious violation of boundaries that would set the stage for later addictive patterns.

Abandonment events such as divorce, death, separations, or being orphaned have frequently happened to sex addicts. They then spend the rest of life trying to complete the grief process. If the process is not done correctly, the incidence of addictive patterns increases dramatically.

Scapegoating or discrediting experiences as a child are also common. A vast majority of addicts will describe their families as being negative, judgmental, and critical during the developmental years. Early on, the child is blamed for many of the problems within the family. Despite any efforts to change, explain, or accommodate, the child was identified as the family symptom-bearer.

A factor common to almost all sex addicts is a fundamental *failure to bond* with the healthy side of another person. There is no nurturing parent who shows the child unconditional love and who is always there to help. Neither is there a rational, problem-solving parent who models and helps the child face up to daily problems and frustrations. The common denominator is a lack of emotional and spiritual connectedness.

Patrick Carnes, in his work on sexual dependency at Golden Valley Health Center in Minnesota, reported that eighty-one percent of the 600 addicts he had surveyed at the time of this report had been sexually abused. Seventy-three percent had been physically abused, and ninety-seven percent had been emotionally abused.[1] These shocking figures emphasize the disastrous effects of *childhood trauma,* and highlight why bonding did not occur and fear of intimacy was present. Because of their victimization, many sex addicts experience humiliation, degradation, and shame as normal. Carnes' findings also suggest that the more abuse the child endures, the more likely there will be multiple addictions.

This victimization creates a double layer of *shame.* There is shame over the abuse experienced as a child. And there is shame over the sexual compulsions and acting out that takes place as an adult. This makes it very difficult to break through the layer of denial. The addict refuses to acknowledge the extent of his lack of control. To do so would mean he would have to deal with truckloads full of shame and guilt. This load of shame means the addict has difficulty being emotionally present during stressful or meaningful times. An example is a father being preoccupied during his child's birthday party, because he is feeling guilty and remorseful about the last acting out episode.

Sexual addiction is an obsession and preoccupation with sex. Everything in the life of the addict is *sexualized.* The language and manner of the addict is likely to be laced with sexual references and innuendoes. The addict will notice sexual connotations in casual conversation, TV programs, and reading material. The sex addict will perceive even innocent and naive persons as sending sexual invitations.

Sexual addiction is a source of pain, confusion, and fear for the addict and the people around her. The compulsion causes her to become progressively dishonest, self-centered, isolated, fearful, confused, devoid of feeling, two-faced, controlling, perfectionistic, blinded to her problem, blaming of others, and dysfunctional.[2]

Like other addictions, sexual addiction is *progressive.* Most sex addicts experience escalating patterns of frequency or intensity of acting out behavior. This happens because the body and emotions recalibrate or adapt to present sexual situations. Prior levels of behavior are no longer able to produce a significant mood change. The person then has to act out more often or find more risque, dangerous, sensuous, or blatant activities.

BELIEF SYSTEM IN SEXUAL ADDICTION

Sexual addiction begins with a delusional thought process. These core beliefs about himself affect how the addict perceives reality. This belief system consists of all the assumptions, judgments, values, and misbeliefs that one holds to be true.

Each of us has a belief system which is our model of the world. On the basis of that belief system, we make decisions, interpret other people's actions, make meaning out of daily experiences, direct our relationships, and establish priorities.

Scripture validates this concept when it says, "For as he thinketh in his heart, so is he" (Proverbs 23:7, KJV); "Do not conform any longer to the pattern of this world, but be transformed by the renewing of your mind" (Romans 12:2a); "I have written both of them as reminders to stimulate you to wholesome thinking" (2 Peter 3:1b).

If the thinking is clear, one's choices will be good. But the addict's belief system contains faulty and inaccurate ideas. The following core beliefs have been found to be almost universally present in the thought processes of addicts:

- I am basically a bad, unworthy person.
- No one would love me as I am.
- My needs are never going to be met if I have to depend on others.
- Sex is my most important need.[3]
- If I have to depend on my social skills to get close to anyone, it will never happen.[4]

The addict concludes from his family experiences that he is not a worthwhile person. Feelings of inadequacy and failure are common. The person sees humiliation and degradation as justified or deserved. The continual struggle with sexual compulsivity serves to confirm this belief and lowers the self-esteem even more. Because of their unworthiness, addicts are committed to hiding the reality of their addiction at all cost. They believe everyone would abandon them if the truth were known.

Addicts have a constant fear of being dependent on others. They perceive their sexual behavior as so bad that everything becomes their fault. They assume responsibility for all the pain in their loved ones. Guilt and remorse cannot be expressed because that would require honesty about behavior. This leads to the addicts becoming progressively more isolated.

A sexual addict feels unloved and unlovable. This means other people cannot be depended on to love him. Therefore, his needs will not be met. The resulting rage and anger become internalized as depression, resentment, self-pity, and even suicidal feelings. Because he has no confidence in the love of others, the addict becomes calculating, strategizing, manipulative, and ruthless. He believes rules and laws are made for people who are lovable, and that those who are unlovable survive in other ways.

The sex addict also confuses nurture and sex. Support, care, affirmation, and love are all sexualized. Absolute terror of life without sex combines with feelings of unworthiness for such intense sexual desires. Sexual activity never meets the need for love and care, but continues to be seen as the only avenue to do so. The addict has a high need to control all situations in an effort to guarantee sex. Yet, there is a secret fear of being sexually out of control. Consequently sexual obsession pervades the addict's lifestyle and behavior.[5]

Finally, the addict is convinced she is not capable of getting close to someone. She believes that she simply does not have the social skills to get the job done. Further, there is no chance of changing or learning how to develop these skills. Besides, since she is such a terrible person, no one wants to accept or love her, so why even try? Now a complete circle has been made in her thinking and the belief system is perpetuated.

These core beliefs lead the addict to other faulty thinking patterns which support the addictive cycle. The resulting sense of being powerless and out of control serves to strengthen the core beliefs. These intensified beliefs activate still more preoccupation with sex, and the addictive system becomes fully engaged. Because sexual behavior is the only thing that makes his isolation bearable, the addict hangs on to it with everything he has.

Out of the belief system comes a distorted view of reality. Denial is the most obvious method of distorting the real world. There are many ways to deny to oneself and others there is a problem. Ignoring, blaming others, and minimizing the behavior are common forms. Argument, excuses, justifications, and circular reasoning abound in the addict's faulty thinking. Examples are:

- If I don't have it every few days, I can't be as efficient at work.
- I am just oversexed, and this is necessary to meet my needs.
- She really enjoyed that and wanted me to do it.
- I deserve it, because I am under so much stress.
- I couldn't help myself. He tempted me more than anybody could be expected to resist.

Whatever the rationalization, it further cuts off the addict from the reality of her behavior. Carnes says that sincere delusion is believing your own lies.[6] An addict will make a very sincere commitment to change her behavior. She will even experience tears of pain, tenderness, or anger when someone doesn't believe her good intentions. However, her promises to others are no more valid than her promises to herself. Feeling sincere about telling a lie is evidence of seriously impaired thinking.[7]

Each delusional thought process—denial, rationalization, sincere delusion, paranoia, and blame—closes off an important avenue of self-discovery for the addict. There is no feedback which would inform him about the inappropriateness of his thinking. He is closed off from the real world and continues within the illusory world of compulsive thoughts.

LEVELS OF SEXUAL ADDICTION
To help understand the escalation of sexual addiction, Carnes has suggested three levels of operation. The first level contains behaviors which are regarded by the general culture as normal, acceptable, or tolerable. Examples would be masturbation, homosexuality, and prostitution. Level Two extends to those behaviors which are clearly victimizing and often illegal. Level Three behaviors have significant negative consequences for the victims and legal implications for the offender. Not every addict progresses from Level One to Level Three. It is possible to be out of control and remain at Level One. However, it would be unusual for a person to be acting out compulsively at Levels Two or Three without having first gone through Level One. Wheth-

er within a given level or across the three, it is important to understand how the behavior spreads to cause more and more destruction.[8]

Level One. Sexual behavior at this level is either accepted or tolerated by society. The primary characteristic is the devastating consequences when the behavior is acted out compulsively. Even the healthiest forms of sexuality can be turned into addiction.

The key building block in compulsive sexuality is the uncontrolled fantasy life that is paired with certain environmental triggers. Fantasizing to masturbation with a nude picture is an example. The sexual release following masturbation becomes associated with both sexual fantasy and the visual cues of a naked body. Sensual objects or sexual thoughts then become precursors to a mood change. It is the anticipation of good feelings that gives sexual situations their potential for addiction.

Acting out can include continual affairs, either ongoing liaisons with one or several persons or a series of one-night stands. Excessive masturbation, pornography, phone sex services, fetishism, bestiality, sadomasochism, strip shows, and prostitution are part of Level One. Also included is sexual behavior in marriage where one person disregards the needs of his partner in the service of his own sexual demands. Demanding sex three times a day in spite of the spouse's desire, is an example. The warning sign here is when one spouse feels victimized by the other's sexual requirements. The problem intensifies when the offending partner dismisses the feelings of the exploited spouse. Any marriage has times when sexual needs are not met and this is not necessarily indicative of an addiction. But when the addict makes his partner a possession or object, a compulsive quality enters the picture. Sex loses its nurturing, fun-loving quality as the relationship becomes empty, joyless, and demoralizing.[9]

A frequent pattern at this level is multiple relationships. The woman who cannot stop the repetition of one-night stands and the man who jumps from one sexual relationship to another, are examples. Love is not present; the motivation is the fear of having to live without sex. The supply must be protected and much thought and effort goes into ensuring that supply.

Cruising is a common type of fix for a Level One addict. Hustling takes place in bars, streets, parties, and even church events. Professional, business, and educational settings can also be prospecting opportunities. The mood change is accomplished by the anticipation: Will I find someone? How will I convey my availability? The addict may recall previous sexual experiences, including the smells, music, sounds, and visual cues that led up to the score.[10]

Sexually oriented magazines, movies, videos, and books are major stepping-stones for sexual addiction. While the human body is a beautiful creation, commercial and addictive interests have almost destroyed any possibility of legitimate art form. Porno shops, x-rated movies, topless and bottomless bars, and erotic art provide a wide array of compulsive samplings. They all offer excitement with a sexual object. The combination is a powerhouse for addictive acting out. No relationship with another person is required. Just look and experience the change in mood.

Visual addiction is almost universal. On any street corner you can find men straining their necks to watch a good-looking woman walking down the street in a short skirt or summer dress. The addict will drive around the block several times looking for the same woman. He will spend hours browsing in an adult bookstore, or sitting on the beach fantasizing sexual activities with the swimmers and sunbathers in skimpy, tight-fitting swimsuits. This powerful attraction will cause the person to drive around college campuses, parks, schools, playgrounds, shopping malls, or other places where there are attractive sex objects. The addict may argue there is no harm in watching. But time and money is misused, work doesn't get done, excuses are made, lies are told, and the progressive erosion of trust and self-esteem continues.

Prostitution has many forms. Call girls, massage parlors, escort services, public relations "consultants," phone sex, and streetwalkers are some of the alternatives. The addict becomes involved with this form of sexual gratification in such a way as to cause himself harm and destruction. Prostitution is an immediate fix, has few entanglements, and is usually anonymous. Yet there is the danger of disease, injury, theft, disclosure, legal penalty, and the consequences of lies. Expense is a significant factor. An addict may spend $100 on a prostitute, and then come home to children who need clothes or school supplies. Even this painful realization does not limit the compulsive behavior.

Another type of Level One addiction involves those who are obsessed with *repressing* sexuality. This includes characteristics such as frigidity, impotence, sexual righteousness, obsessive sexual purity, nonintegrated celibacy, religious sexual obsession, and sexual anorexia. While the theme of these characteristics is the denial, repression, or avoidance of sex, the outcome is similar to acting out. Sexual thoughts become the dominant force in the person's life until he is preoccupied with sex. But in this case, the preoccupation is the compulsive avoidance of sexual thoughts or behavior. These forms of denial can be just as destructive as sexual acting out.[11]

Level Two. The addictive behavior in this level extends to behaviors which are clearly victimizing and sufficiently intrusive of others to warrant legal sanctions. These nuisance offenses include exhibitionism, indecent phone calls, indecent liberties, and voyeurism. Enforcement of these violations vary. Yet there are clearly victims and there are sanctions. It is precisely the fact of doing something risky that makes the sexual activity all the more attractive. It makes for a better "fix."

The stereotype of an exhibitionist or flasher is somebody who wears a wide-brimmed hat and a dark raincoat on a sunny day, and lurks in dark corners of a playground. Actually, exhibitionists are quite varied in their methods. Some will drive their cars with their pants pulled down. Others will leave their pants zipper open while standing in an elevator or phone booth. Some will have a "strategic" hole in their pants, or wear intentionally revealing clothing. Another method is to leave curtains "inadvertently" ajar in the bedroom or bathroom. Ringing a doorbell and exposing when it is answered is a more dramatic and risky option for others.

Exhibitionists lead double lives, fearful that someone will recognize them. Self-condemnation is prevalent. The addict judges himself as weird or perverted, but lacks the ability to change.

Voyeurism and exhibitionism often go together. The connecting link is masturbation. For the voyeur, masturbating while watching a person undress is another way of enhancing the excitement.[12]

The voyeur is sustained by excitement. He waits in a trancelike state, sometimes for hours, in uncomfortable conditions, for a few seconds of nudity. Totally absorbed with the anticipation of the moment, he loses all contact with reality. Cares, worries, work or family responsibilities, and financial problems are all forgotten. He could go to the nearest topless bar and see more skin with less risk, but it would not be the same. The mood-altering qualities of the experience are enhanced by the intrusive, secretive, stolen parts of the behavioral sequence.[13]

Where voyeurism is a visual form of victimization, the indecent phone call is the auditory version. Addicts report masturbation is an important link here also. They start by masturbating while talking on the phone. Soon, however, the behavior must become more explicit for it to have any affect.

Indecent liberties are inappropriate touches. The victim knows she has been touched or fondled, but has not given permission. The addict plans how to "accidentally" touch a breast or thigh in a crowded bus or elevator. The addict knows he is committing a criminal act and that only serves to fuel the compulsion. All the same ingredients are present: the stolen, the illicit, the exciting.

Having transgressed personal boundaries at one level, the progressive nature of addiction propels the addict into needing more explicit and dangerous experiences. This leads to Level Three behavior.

Level Three. The compulsive behavior at this level has significant negative consequences for the victim and legal implications for the offender. The common element in this level is the violation of some of society's most significant boundaries — crimes such as rape, incest, and molestation. Participation at this level shows a severe progression of the addiction.

A distinction between sociopathic and addictive offenders needs to be made. For offenses such as rape, molestation, and incest, sociopaths are unaware of wrongdoing and appear to have no conscience. They blunt any sense of guilt by blaming others, believing that society owes them certain rights to sexual satisfaction, or that the victim really wanted the offense to take place. The addict who commits rape, molestation, or child sexual abuse does feel guilt, but is caught up in the compulsion to repeat the cycle anyway. Both types are guilty of a crime, but there is a different sense of responsibility and remorse in favor of the addict.

CYCLE OF SEXUAL ADDICTION

The experience of the sexual addict progresses through a four-step cycle which intensifies with each repetition. These steps are preoccupation, ritualization, compulsive sexual behavior, and despair.

Preoccupation. Because the addict's mind is completely engrossed with thoughts and fantasies of sex, every encounter is passed through a sexually obsessive filter. People become objects to be scrutinized as this trancelike mental state creates an obsessive search for sexual stimulation. The addict is like a hostage to this obsession. Every passerby, every relationship, every encounter must pass through the sexually obsessive filter. People become objects to be scrutinized. A walk through a shopping mall becomes a veritable shopping spree for making visual contacts with possibilities.

Think of the intoxicating oneness of two lovers who are so absorbed in one another they are oblivious to their surroundings. The addict is after the same intoxication. It is the hunt, the suspense, the pursuit of the stolen and forbidden that make the experience intoxicating.[14]

The addict's mood is altered as she enters the obsessive trance. The physiological process is stimulated as adrenaline speeds up the body's functioning. The heart pounds as the addict focuses on her mood-altering object or experience. Risk, danger, and violence are guaranteed escalators. Preoccupation serves to dull any warnings of personal pain, remorse, or guilt. The addict does not always have to act; often, just thinking about prior activity brings relief.

Ritualization. A ritual helps the trance. The ritual itself can enhance the rush of excitement. A ritual is the addict's special routine which leads up to the sexual behavior. The ritual intensifies the preoccupation, adding arousal and excitement.

The rituals contain a set of well-rehearsed cues which trigger arousal. The preoccupation trance and the extensive rituals are as important, or sometimes more important, than the sexual contact. The anticipatory rituals make the whole process more intoxicating. One cannot be orgasmic all the time, so the search and suspense absorb the addict's concentration and energy. Cruising, watching, waiting, and preparing are part of the mood alteration.

Compulsive sexual behavior. This is the actual sexual act which is the goal of the preoccupation and ritualization.

At this point the addict is unable to control his behavior. In spite of prior resolves to stop, the addict is powerless. He has lost control over his sexual thoughts and behavior.

Despair. The feeling of utter hopelessness addicts have about their behavior and their powerlessness is the low phase of the four-step cycle. It occurs after the addict has been compulsively sexual. The feeling includes a sense of failure for not keeping the resolutions to stop, along with hopelessness about ever being able to control the behavior. He may also experience self-pity and self-hatred, and in the extreme, may contemplate suicide.

This cycle repeats itself because the ever-ready preoccupation can be used to bring the addict out of the pit of despair. This makes the cycle self-perpetuating. Each new repetition adds to the previous experiences and solidifies the cyclic nature of the addiction. As the struggle continues, the addict's life will start to disintegrate and become unmanageable. Within this addictive system, sexual experience becomes the reason for living, the primary relationship. The phases of behavior which lead to an altered state of consciousness make normal sexual behavior tame by comparison. This cycle is the energizing force within the addiction.[15]

EFFORTS TO CONTROL SEXUAL ADDICTION

Many sex addicts have used excessive religiosity as a way to control their behavior. They may make spiritual vows, engage in seemingly earnest prayers, and attend church services continuously. Their compulsive personality latches on to religious activity with the same strength as it did to their sexual acting out. Now they have at least two separate addictions tearing away at them.

An important distinction needs to be made here between trying to do it ourselves and letting God work in our lives. There is tremendous power and hope in our faith in God. God has promised to help and strengthen us when we need it (Psalms 28:7; 40:17; Isaiah 41:10). He has promised to show us the way out of difficult places (Isaiah 30:21; 42:16). Our Lord has promised to remove obstacles from our lives (Isaiah 40:4; 45:2; Matthew 21:21) and to answer our prayers (Psalm 91:15; Isaiah 58:9; Luke 11:9; John 15:7).

All of these promises are true. But what about the countless people whose lives are out of control? Why haven't their earnest prayers been answered? I don't propose to have an easy answer to this difficult question. But there is a significant difference between expecting religious behavior and piety to effect a release from addiction, and letting go of all pretense that we can do anything to gain our freedom. The key is surrender. We must trust in the Lord and not in ourselves. His guidance will straighten our path (Proverbs 3:5-6). We must decide to give ourselves to Him, and then follow His direction.

Those who compulsively, yet sincerely, turn to religious activity are operating from a belief that their own actions will be successful. This won't work. We must be weak, in order to be made strong (2 Corinthians 12:9-10). All God asks is that we turn our lives over to Him, acknowledging our failures, and look to Him for direction and strength. This is not a one-time act, for each day must be a new commitment. There are times when we think we can do a better job ourselves, take back the control, and crash and burn. Learning to trust God takes us on a long and difficult journey.

Other forms of control have been attempted by sex addicts—changing jobs or moving to another region in order to "start over." They may seek therapy with varying results. If the core issues are not resolved, the exact nature of their sexual addiction identified, and appropriate treatment provided, they will not be helped.

SELF-EVALUATION
Truthfully answer the following questions to see if sexual compulsion could be a significant part of your life.

TEST FOR SEXUAL ADDICTION

_____ 1. Do you look to sexual experiences or thoughts to help you deal with many of the daily pressures of life?

_____ 2. Do you spend a portion of almost every day thinking about how your sexual needs will be met?

_____ 3. Do you spend significant amounts of time in activities related to obtaining sexual experiences or in recovering from episodes of being sexual?

_____ 4. Have you had numerous occasions where either the amount, duration, or extent of your sexual activity exceeded what you intended to happen?

_____ 5. Have you noticed significant mood shifts, as from depression to excitement or vice versa, when you become sexual?

___ 6. Have you had to increase your sexual activity in order to at least maintain former levels of enjoyment?

___ 7. Have you engaged in activities that are dangerous or risky in order to find sexual gratification?

___ 8. Have you tried to stop or limit your sexual behavior with little or no success?

___ 9. Have you been unable to stop acting out in sexual ways, in spite of adverse consequences that have affected your health, job, relationships with friends and/or family, finances, or legal status?

___ 10. Have you struggled with feeling out of control of your sexual behavior for at least two years?

___ 11. Over at least the past five years, have you experienced periods of both extreme self-control and being out of control in regard to your sexual behavior?

___ 12. Have you suffered severe consequences as a result of your sexual behavior?

___ 13. Do you have a clear order of preferences for your most enjoyable to least enjoyable sexual experiences?

___ 14. Have you altered or sacrificed certain social, occupational, or recreational activities in order to devote time to your sexual interests?

___ 15. Answer yes if you have experienced two or more of the following:
   a. Shame about your activities
   b. Depression
   c. Other addictions
   d. A victim of sexual abuse, previously or currently
   e. A victim of emotional or physical abuse, previously or currently
   f. A secret double life due to your sexual behavior
   g. A belief that nurturance and love is sexual
   h. Few or no nonsexual relationships
   i. Suicidal thoughts or attempts
   j. A tendency to deny the existence of a problem
   k. The presence of a codependent relationship, or romance addictive personality[16]

If you answered yes to five or more of the above items, you very likely are struggling with a sexual addiction. If you had fewer than five positive responses, it doesn't mean you have never struggled with your sexuality. Look at the specific items you did answer positively and see if any type of pattern emerges. You have to judge your degree of honesty about the questions. Remember denial is the first hurdle to overcome in regaining control.

WHAT TO DO?

The following personal story illustrates the characteristics, progression, and devastation of sexual addiction. It also demonstrates some of the key components of recovery.

Gene had learned very early in life how to avoid the pain of reality—he would retreat to fantasy and sexual preoccupation. As far back as he could remember, Gene was lonely and fearful. So he became very skilled at using one of these pathways to escape the frustrations of day-to-day existence.

His sexual addiction began in childhood with frequent masturbation and some pornographic magazines he found in a trash bin. Gene also sought out anything in magazines, newspapers, or TV that would serve as a sexual trigger. There was always a burden of shame, and Gene lived in constant dread of the prospect of his family finding out about his sexual obsessions and behavior.

Adolescence was a time of tremendous conflict and emotional pressure for Gene. While he seldom dated, he constantly fantasized about sexual activities with girls. At the same time, he struggled to rid himself of the continual preoccupation with sex, but told no one about his dilemma.

Gene attended college away from home so was able to more freely engage in his sexual acting out. He started attending x-rated movies and porno shops in the college town where he lived. He always did these things with constant fear that he would be seen by someone he knew.

Gene became a Christian during his college days and tried repeatedly to gain control of his sexual preoccupation, because he knew God did not approve. Yet it seemed the harder he tried, the more intense was the need to cover his guilt with yet more sexual acting out. When Gene did date during college, his motives were always sexual. After each conquest, remorse overwhelmed him. But in a few days the pressure would begin to build and Gene would make another "hit."

There were several traumatic encounters with girls who either accused Gene of date rape or threatened to do something drastic if he didn't continue to see them. He managed to avoid any lasting repercussions, but the emotional pressure only served as a stimulus to engage in more sexual behavior in order to escape the pain. It was a vicious and constant destructive cycle.

After college Gene began a career in sales. The nature of his work allowed him access to many sexual partners as well as the freedom to check out the skin flicks and adult bookstores in each city within his territory. Each time Gene bought a porno book or rented an x-rated video, he swore to himself it would never happen again. But, eventually, the cycle would repeat itself.

Gene met a wonderful girl through his work, and they eventually married. Things seemed better for a while. They became involved in a church, had a child, and Gene's career prospered. But after a couple of years, Gene started an extramarital affair that lasted for about six months. During that period he would do anything to maintain his access to his mistress and the illicit sexual activity.

The internal pressures were tremendous. For example, Gene would buy his mistress lavish gifts to ensure sexual favors and then have to cover up his expenditures, jeopardizing his financial security. He had to lie to his wife and employer to cover his trail of risks, late-night encounters, and unexplained absences. The stress heightened to such a point that Gene finally sought help. He started seeing a counselor who suggested Gene might be a sexual addict. Gene strongly denied the assessment. After all, he wasn't some kind of weirdo who lurked in dark corners waiting to molest children.

Gene did start attending a support group for men in distress and after about three months of individual therapy was able to break off the affair. Soon after, Gene told his counselor about his attendance at a work-related workshop. During that entire weekend Gene was constantly preoccupied with sexual thoughts and urges. His life wasn't particularly stressful at that time, and he couldn't understand why he was so preoccupied with sex. It felt like an obsession, and Gene was frightened by his lack of self-control. The counselor restated his belief that Gene was powerless over his sexual thoughts and behaviors and thus qualified as a sexual addict. He believed Gene was not able to control when he started or stopped his sexual behavior, in spite of negative and harmful consequences. Finally, the denial was broken. Gene admitted he was addicted to sex.

At the urging of the counselor, Gene started attending a

Twelve Step group for sex addicts. He was resistant at first. After all, Gene thought, he had never been arrested or done anything terribly illegal. But after the initial sessions, Gene knew he had found a safe place to reveal his feelings and thoughts without fear of recrimination. The group was made up of other people just like Gene. He learned to respect the honesty and courage of the men and women in the group. With their help, Gene was able to turn away from a life dominated by shame and secrecy. In its place he began to experience more self-respect and honesty.

Gene's recovery was gradual, at times frustrating, but progressive. His initial goals were to stop using all forms of pornography and to end the habit of masturbating with the use of pornographic or sexual fantasy as a stimulus. Gene found he was even tempted to act out by looking at covers of magazines or ads in the newspapers. He learned to draw clear boundaries regarding these behaviors. He found he had to avoid contact with sexually oriented ads, movies, or TV. For example, Gene would use the remote control on his TV to scan the channels for sexually oriented scenes. When this happened, Gene knew his addiction was looking for a fix.

Gene also had to learn to deal with the thousands of images he carried in his memory from his pornographic exposure and a lifetime of sexual encounters. His addictive nature enjoyed remembering or reliving those stimulating images and experiences. He had to learn how to end that obsessive behavior by using thought-stopping techniques, prayer, memorizing of Scripture, Christian music, or talking to his sponsor, wife, or prayer partner.

Gene's wife also entered into the counseling process and dealt with her feelings of betrayal and anger. They also spent time in couple therapy. Gradually, through many attempts and some relapses, Gene was able to regain control of his life. His thinking pattern began to change. His unrealistic expectations for himself and others began to modify. He was able to trust people more and to enjoy true intimacy with his wife and family. The shroud of secrecy and deceit was stripped away. With the help of his counselor and others, Gene was able to accept his own shortcomings as well as the limitations of others. He began to see he was a person worth loving and that there was no longer the need to escape the pain of shame by sexual acting out.

Gene continues to ask God daily to help him stay sober; on his own, he will not be able to maintain control. But God is answering Gene's prayers by providing the power to work through the negative feelings and help maintain his road to recovery. Gene has a new life, and for that he is most grateful.

Gene's story illustrates many of the characteristics of sexual addiction described earlier — the use of sex to avoid intimacy and feelings. Because his belief system was faulty, sex became his most important need. Gene's behavior remained at Level One, although adultery clearly has its victims.

The cycle of addiction was also present. He was preoccupied with sex, spent large amounts of time planning how to get sex, acted out, and felt remorse and depression afterward.

But Gene's story also shows some of the key elements of recovery. Like any form of addiction, he had to surrender control of his life. He had to acknowledge his powerlessness to his addiction.

Second, he entered into a counseling process. Often there are significant issues of the family of origin that can be worked out only in therapy. Common themes of abandonment, abuse, anger, resentment, damaged goods, shame, guilt, forgiveness, and self-identity are important topics for the counseling process. A skilled therapist can help uncover and process feelings that may have been buried for years.

It is important to select a therapist who understands sexual addiction. Feel free to ask a potential therapist about his or her qualifications and experience. You will also want to meet with a counselor once or twice and see how the interaction goes. It is crucial to feel comfortable with your counselor. Don't expect him or her to be perfect. But a comfortable match is necessary.

Gene also entered a Twelve Step program for those with a similar addiction. The empathy, support, instruction, and shared accountability of such a group has frequently been of immense value in recovery and maintaining sobriety. Such a support group should accompany the counseling component at some point. Both are necessary; neither is sufficient in and of itself. Addiction is powerful and insidious, and the depth of individual counseling and the support of a group are both needed to facilitate recovery.

An important part of recovery is abstinence. At some critical point you must make the decision to stop acting out. This certainly includes all forms of inappropriate sexual acting out. Many addicts have found, even though they were married, it was necessary to refrain from all forms of sexual behavior for a certain period. It is a form of sexual detoxification. For most addicts, lust has predominated until they are possessed and controlled by it. Whether married or not, addicts are poisoned by the compulsion. A period of voluntary sexual abstinence can be a way of taking inventory of yourself and your relationship. In the beginning stages of sobriety, it may be hard for the addict to separate lust or compulsive sex from the healthy and sacred form of sexual expression that God intended. Abstinence is a way of uncovering unhealthy motives and learning to relate to your spouse in nonsexual ways. It can be a time of improving communication and expanding your expressions of love. A period of abstinence should be entered into with the understanding of your mate, and with a clear purpose in mind. Your counselor or sponsor should also be involved to assist you in achieving the desired results.

Release from the bondage of sexual addiction must include the reversal of the feelings of alienation and self-hate. Gene found roots in a caring community. With this assistance he was able to begin developing new beliefs about himself and to get rid of dysfunctional thinking. A crucial process in overcoming an addiction is to replace faulty beliefs with healthy ones. The core beliefs described earlier can be replaced by these:

- I am a worthwhile person deserving of pride.
- I am loved and accepted by people who know me as I am.
- My needs can be met by others if I let them know what those needs are.
- Sex is but one expression of my need and concern for others.[17]
- I can learn to relate on an intimate, but nonsexual, basis with another person.

Counseling, support groups, involvement in a caring community, and the following of a Twelve Step program can all contribute to the learning of these healthy core beliefs. If you wish to locate a Twelve Step group or professional counseling, check with your pastor, Christian counseling services, or community service referral organizations such as the Crisis Clinic. Several national headquarters for Twelve Step groups are given in the resource section of this book. Remember to follow the six-meeting rule in checking out a support group. Attend the meetings regularly at least six times, before deciding about your participation. There are strong forces within you to suggest many reasons for not staying with a certain group. Many of the reasons are merely forms of denial. Keep hanging in there. It's tremendously hard work, but it's worth it.

Professional group therapy provides a safe place for you to learn to communicate and relate to others under the guidance of a mental health professional. Because a therapist is present to serve as a facilitator, guide, and teacher, it is a good place to take significant emotional risks and learn how to relate. A support group may give you persons to call on any time of the day—something that may not be true of a therapy group. But your therapist can help you acquire specific insight into your addictive cycle. Group therapy can also help you examine your belief system and ways of thinking, which significantly contribute to your self-esteem. These groups are offered by counseling centers and community mental health centers, as well as private practitioners.

Family and couple therapy can be another important ingredient in recovery. Addiction is often a generational and family problem. Issues such as codependency, relationship addiction, family denial, lack of trust, distorted communication, and expression of anger are often topics covered with a recovering couple or family.

The intellectual side of you can be stimulated by classes, workshops, seminars, and books. These things do not replace therapy and support groups, but they can serve as meaningful supplements to the recovery process. Attending conferences on addictions or various aspects of the recovery or healing process can be enlightening and encouraging. There is an increasing number of books on the topic of addictions, including workbooks on the Twelve Steps. See the reference section for suggestions.

A caring community is crucial. I hope this will include your church. However, sex has an inordinately bad reputation within the church. Any kind of sexual sin carries a high level of penance and criticism. Because of this, it may be difficult to reveal much of your struggle. As more of our church constituency becomes better educated about addictions, the better able pastors and church members will be to help minister in this area.

A church does provide an opportunity to worship and praise God, as well as fellowship. These are crucial opportunities for the recovering addict. The spiritual dimension needs careful attention, and the local congregation has unique potential to help. No church is perfect, but many are excellent spiritual hospitals for those with emotional and spiritual injuries. Become a part of one where you find acceptance along with accountability.

Take care of your physical needs. If your acting out has involved any kind of sexual contact, you and your mate should have a complete screening for sexually transmitted diseases. Consult a gynecologist, urologist, or other appropriate specialist in infectious diseases. It is far better to allay or confirm fears about having contacted a disease because of your addiction, than to avoid dealing with the possibility. The alternative is an untreated harmful or deadly affliction with potentially fatal consequences.

Another dimension of your physical being is exercise and diet. Physical activity can be a healthy alternative to compulsive sexual acting out. It can also help you feel better and help build up a body that probably has been neglected. Watch what you eat. It can be all too easy to stop your sexual behavior only to substitute a craving for food. Eat healthy foods. I know I sound like your mother, but the advice is correct!

Finally, develop a balanced recreation program. Everyone needs to play once in a while. To help turn your attention away from sex, learn some new hobbies. Pick up old interests that you ignored as sex took up more of your time and resources. Learn how to have fun again, but in ways that are not compulsive.

Your recovery will likely not follow a straight path. Slipping back into old patterns is very common. But do not interpret a single error as a total failure. Don't get into the faulty thinking that a failure takes you back to square one. Recurrence of compulsive behavior does not mean you are a total disaster. You will have made some growth in your recovery, and you can continue to do so if you don't let feelings of failure overwhelm your positive gains.

On the other hand, just because error is common, don't give yourself permission to fail. Recovery is hard, and slips are possible. But don't use that possibility to talk yourself into probability thinking. Choose to be free of your obsession with sex. Do everything, with God's power, to overcome your addiction. Do not use the possibility of setbacks as a justification of continuing addictive acting out. A related caution is not to turn a failure into a binge. Faulty thinking could say, "I've already messed up, so I might as well go for the rest of it." Sure, it's discouraging to fall; but, rather than make things worse, pick yourself up and get back on that horse. Ask forgiveness, make restitution and amends where you have offended or hurt someone, learn from your mistake, and get on with the recovery. Recovery does not demand perfection.

N O T E S

1. Mark Laaser, "Diagnosis and Treatment of Sexual Addictions," presented at International Congress on Christian Counseling, Atlanta, Georgia, November 9–13, 1988.
2. Anne Wilson Schaef, *Escape from Intimacy* (New York: Harper & Row), 1989, 11.
3. Patrick Carnes, *Out of the Shadows* (Minneapolis: CompCare Publishers), 1983, 77–80, 135.
4. Ralph Earle and Gregory Crow, *Lonely All the Time* (New York: Pocket Books), 1989, 19.
5. Carnes, *Out of the Shadows*, 82–85.
6. *Ibid.*, 7.
7. *Ibid.*, 7.
8. *Ibid.*, 27.
9. *Ibid.*, 30.
10. *Ibid.*, 30.
11. Schaef, *Escape from Intimacy*, 32.
12. Carnes, *Out of the Shadows*, 41.
13. *Ibid.*, 40.
14. *Ibid.*, 10.
15. *Ibid.*, 12.
16. Laaser, "Diagnosis and Treatment of Sexual Addictions."
17. Carnes, *Out of the Shadows*, 138.

CHAPTER FIVE

EATING ADDICTION
Are Your Thoughts Consumed with Food?

● It seems harmless enough — it's only a box of doughnuts. But that box of flour and sugar has the power to control millions of people. We might think of the doughnut as a delicious morsel unable to defend itself from the ravishing assault of a human junk food disposal. But for countless persons that box of tasty treats has the power of a hundred armies. For those with an eating addiction, food has the power to control and determine behavior.

If the person spying the box of bakery goodies is an anorexic, she might react with fear over gaining a pound just by smelling them, even though she might be severely underweight.

A bulimic individual might see the doughnuts and wolf down the entire box in five minutes, in spite of being 100 pounds overweight, only to intentionally throw it all up half an hour later.

An overeater might take an entire afternoon to alternately eat half of a doughnut, close the box, work around the kitchen, then eat another half, until the box is empty.

How can food get this much power? It happens in the same way as with drugs, alcohol, relationships, or sex. The food addict uses food to cope with negative feelings and stressful situations. For many, loving food is safer than loving people. Eating is a very intimate experience. When we eat, a foreign substance is brought within our personal boundaries and made a part of our very essence. A pepperoni pizza enters our system, is digested, and made into living cells. It is a form of unity unmatched by any other relationship. In our desire to find intimacy, we turn to food because it is far easier to control and more predictable than people. Besides, it tastes good!

As many as sixty to eighty million Americans may be affected by some form of eating disorders. A recent Gallup Poll indicated that one in eight teenage girls is battling an eating disorder. The same survey found that up to one-fourth of women from ages nineteen to thirty-nine have periodically gone on food binges. Half of them have then resorted to extreme measures, like fasting or self-induced vomiting, to keep themselves from gaining weight.[1]

Other studies report that forty percent of all Americans compulsively overeat.[2] Preoccupation with weight loss has spawned an industry that, by one count several years ago, promoted 28,096 weight-reducing methods and gadgets, of which no more than six percent were judged by experts to be safe and effective.[3]

One estimate is that the dieting industry accounts for ten billion dollars a year in expenditures.[4] Take your pick of fad diets—the ice cream diet, grapefruit diet, drinking man's diet, rice diet, high carbohydrate diets, high protein diets, balanced diets, or Pritikin. Every one of these has worked, to some degree, with someone; but none of them work with everyone. And besides, diets don't work unless there is a dramatic change in the relationship between the person and the food.

Like any addiction, eating has dual consequences. One is the physical result to the body of being overfed, starved, undernourished, and brutalized by crash diets and subsequent weight gain. It has been observed that overeating costs the average individual one year of life. Each pound over the ideal weight range will cost a person one month of life.[5]

The second consequence, of course, is the psychic burden of guilt, shame, remorse, and low self-esteem associated with being fat, bulimic, anorexic, or out of control. The self-hatred that comes with being fat, in a culture that gives lip service to the notion that fat is repulsive, is devastating. Whatever the outward demeanor, the person struggling with food control is feeling pain.

While many addictions such as drinking, gambling, or sex can be acted out in private, the affects of overeating are public. You can't hide the facts of fat. Also, total abstinence is not an option for food addiction. We must eat, where alcohol and substance abuse can be totally avoided. This makes recovery much more difficult, because the addict must learn to manage the source of his or her addiction while participating on a daily basis.

PATTERNS OF OVEREATING

Extra weight is gained by eating in excess of the body's need for calories. But not all overeating happens in the same way. Because awareness is always the first step in recovery, it may be helpful to highlight the three types of overeating that have been identified.[6]

Social overeating. Some types of obesity result from overeating high calorie food in a food oriented social environment. Have you noticed how many social invitations occur over the promise of a meal? "Hey, we ought to get together for lunch sometime" is repeated thousands of times a day in our culture. Look at how many church functions involve a meal. We have ladies' luncheons, men's prayer breakfasts, mother-daughter teas, father-son banquets, missionary dinners, etc. Can you imagine hosting a Bible study, support group, or meeting without giving some thought to refreshments? With our cultural emphasis on food as a common denominator for social interaction, it's a wonder all of us are not overweight.

Whether it's a businessperson's lunch, or an award banquet for Little League baseball players, we orchestrate much of our life around food. It's no surprise, then, that a great deal of overeating takes place in the "normal" process of social participation.

Nighttime eating. Persons with this pattern are generally "good" all day long. They have little desire for food and do not overindulge. In the evening, however, they have long eating episodes that end only when they fall asleep. There is usually agitation, anxiety, and insomnia along with this pattern. The next day, the person eats nothing in the morning, very little during the day and overeats, again, in the evening.

Binge eating. Food binges are the ingestion of enormous quantities of food at a very fast pace. A binge is neither a social event nor a celebration. It can happen standing by the sink or walking down the street. The binge is a totally uncontrolled, seizure-like experience. The person often reports feeling dissociated from his behavior. There is a compulsion to eat until the stomach is more than full, even in pain.

Following the death of a twenty-two-year-old woman from the medical complications of repeated binges, her parents found containers in her desk drawer, including a box of one dozen doughnuts, a box of Kentucky Fried Chicken, two empty pizza containers, two empty half-gallon containers of milk, one empty box of cookies, one empty double bag of potato chips, and numerous candy bar wrappers. This young lady had completed a binge of major proportions.[7]

WHY DIETS DON'T WORK

Most diets appear to work relatively well as long as people follow them. The rate and amount of weight loss depends mostly on the degree of caloric restriction. The fewer the calories taken in, the more drastic the weight loss. The reasons diets don't work in the long run is because people sabotage the diet and resume their old eating habits.

The only way to take off weight and keep it off is to change the way we eat. We change the way we eat by understanding the patterns that got us into trouble and then developing new and better ways to cope with life.

A compulsive attraction to food will cause the addict to continue the destructive forms of eating rather than develop healthy ones. Addiction is like a giant snowball rolling down the mountainside. Once it gets going it is very hard to stop. It has a momentum of its own and tends to get worse.

To help in slowing down the snowball and reversing the destructive progression, we need to see how compulsive eating services our needs.

FUNCTION OF COMPULSIVE EATING

There are certain general functions or purposes that may apply to all types of compulsions about food. The major question is, "What do you gain as a result of a compulsive relationship with food?"

First of all, a compulsive attraction to food is *safer and quicker* than looking to people for love and fulfillment. People can be disappointing. Also, they can't get inside your head and instantly know what you need and when you need it. To avoid that disappointment, food is used to provide instant and manageable gratification. This makes the addict very self-sufficient, since the ability to create a change in mood is totally within his control. He doesn't need anybody else. While eating, nothing else matters, and he feels safe and secure. By denying his neediness and seeking comfort in food, he has found a way to stay in control.

Anorexia can be a way of saying, "I don't need people, and I don't need food. I am so self-sufficient I can live on air. I do not need anything!"[8]

A second function of food addiction is that it helps *avoid the risks* of daily living. For a food addict, food becomes a love object. But it serves as both your nurturer and judge. Food gives you an emotional fix when everything else fails, but addiction to food also keeps you imprisoned. Freedom of choice is taken from you. You are not free to make choices, because you're preoccupied with maintaining the food supply. And the emotional and physical consequences of the addiction limit your options.

Eating can be a way to *diminish the disappointment* of not being appreciated. A child who can't please her parents, the wife whose husband no longer gives her compliments, or the man who has been passed over for a promotion—all are candidates for using food to help handle the discouragement and lack of appreciation.

Food is *familiar* and its effects are constant and predictable. Change can be terrifying. Taking risks can bring feelings of awkwardness and anxiety. Compulsive eating can have the same effect as gulping down a few drinks before a crucial job assignment or attending a stressful meeting.

Often eating is a way to *relax* and settle the tensions of life. It can have the tranquilizing effects of sex for an adult, or the thumb-sucking and blanket-tugging of a small child. Food can be a pacifier or security blanket to the child within each of us. Life gets pretty hectic. The pace is bewildering. One solution is to eat and let the chemical reactions of the body provide a soothing respite.

Food becomes a *ritual*. Much of our eating is habitual. The clock strikes twelve and it's time for lunch. Whether our body needs any nourishment or not, we're out the door and off to the cafeteria. We become conditioned to eat at certain times and in certain situations.

Food can be a source for *dealing with our anger*. Have you ever been angry and pulled out a bag of crunchy potato chips or Fritos? You wanted something that crunched, made noise, and exercised the jaws. Ice cream or pudding wouldn't do. It took something noisy and brittle to give sufficient intensity to your feelings.

Food can be used for dealing with other feelings as well. If depressed, we may want a hot fudge sundae. When anxious, a bowl of soup may hit the spot. Everybody has their own preferences, but food can be that ever available relief for distraught feelings.

CHARACTERISTICS OF EATING DISORDERS

Dr. Ray Vath, a specialist in the treatment of anorexia nervosa and bulimia, has identified several characteristics common to all food compulsions. These can help identify the presence of an addictive relationship with food, and also point to topics that must be addressed in recovery.[9]

Perfectionism. Most food addicts have high and unreasonable expectations for themselves. They have definite goals, rules, and plans they use to grade themselves, and they seldom measure up. They are never quite good enough. Food becomes a way of deadening the pain of unmet goals and expectations. An underlying belief that fuels the perfectionism is, "I won't be loved unless I am perfect." The addict lives in a society which places a premium on performance. It's not personhood that is valued so much as a job title, bank account, or square footage of a house. This sets the person up to be a victim of conditional love: "You are valuable only if you are good and achieve to the level other people think you should." This reinforces the other belief of having to be perfect to be loved, and sets the stage for the compulsive cycle to escape disappointment.

Low self-esteem. Because the standards she sets for herself are impossible to meet, the addict feels worthless, inferior, and ineffectual in most areas of her life. Because there is some control attained through the rituals and compulsive behavior around food, this area takes on significant value. This is one reason why the anorexic feels so good when she has lost another pound. She was successful in this one area in contrast to the failures everywhere else. A person with any kind of eating problem has some level of awareness that her eating pattern is out of control. Therefore, she doesn't have the freedom to share her victories. It isn't really a healthy victory and this, again, supports her label of herself as inferior.

Sexual identity confusion. Along with addicts' low self-image is confusion about who they are and how their personhood is going to unfold. This can include the idea that the ideal woman should be thin, and that "Thin is beautiful." But this only deals with the physical dimension of womanhood. A much more important issue than how they look is who they really are. Their idea of what it means to be a man or woman is confused.

Some people believe that the sexual identity of a girl is greatly influenced by the approval of her father and a boy by his mother. Their assumption is that if unhealthy models or lack of approval exist, the resulting sexual identity will be hampered. A preoccupation with food is one way to cope with this incomplete understanding of who the addict is as a male or female being.

Depression. Because of the difference between his unrealistic goals and his performance, the food addict is likely to become depressed. There is also the strong possibility of a family history of depression surrounding the one with the attraction to food. We also know that depression can be an internalized form of anger. There are many things the addict can be angry about: unrealized goals, dysfunctional family members, victimization, an unprotective God, or an unloving spouse. Of course, there are many other sources of anger. But whatever the source, the intense feelings of frustration can be turned toward oneself, creating depression, and assisting the addict to turn to food for security, comfort, and temporary contentment.

Deception. The person with an eating disorder will go to great lengths to hide his behavior. Secrecy and deception are done to prevent his out-of-control behavior from being known. He will eat in private, binge at night, pretend to eat when he does not, steal food, use laxatives, or throw up when no one else is around.

Vath points out how this dishonesty creates an impasse in the person's life. Because he has lied so often to others, he continually fears he is being deceived. This makes it hard to accept the information, recommendations, or treatment of even authority figures like his doctor.[10]

We learned earlier that several addictions tend to cluster together. Both anorexic and bulimic individuals have a high incidence of shoplifting, drug or alcohol abuse. When these behaviors are present, the addict has another level of deception to maintain to avoid being caught or identified.

Struggle for power. Many of my clients who have struggled with eating problems say the criticism about their weight started when they were a child and continued through adulthood. The power struggle in the family starts when the symptoms of the addiction become public. The family tries to force the person to change, employing threats, bribes, cajoling, or punishment in what becomes a struggle for power. Often my clients report that their family members would try to lessen the negative effect of their harassment by saying, "Honey, we wouldn't give you such a bad time if we didn't love you so much." Somehow that type of message comes across as a monstrous contradiction, even though there is some truth to the statement.

Food addiction often occurs in families which are action-oriented. When the problem becomes public, the family tends to jump in to help get things resolved. Rather than taking time to listen and understand how the behavior got out of control, they tend to propose solutions which the addict resists.

Guilt is a major weapon in this struggle. The parent may tell an anorexic daughter, "How can you do this to us? You are upsetting the entire family. Your father is about to lose his job because he is so worried about you." Part of the daughter wants to be compliant to the parental request, and another part resists. As a result more internal tension is created for the addict, and more self-punishment is inflicted. The anorexic continues to not eat or the bulimic overeats. The family feels more victimized and tries to make things better, and the vicious cycle continues.[11]

Interdependency. In many families where eating disorders develop, the parents want to do everything possible to make their child perfect. With this strong desire to see their own unmet goals realized through their child, the parents may have difficulty letting go. When the child moves into the period of emancipation during the late teenage years, problems can occur. The eager-to-please child wants to break away but doesn't know how, and he is afraid. He knows he is out of control. He hopes his family can help him, but he also wants independence and autonomy. He wants to grow up, but is afraid he will mess up his adult life, just like he has mismanaged his health.

The issue is responsibility. The parents of many food addicts have tried to take too much responsibility for orchestrating their child's development, while others have not taken enough. The result is confused messages about who is going to take control of the addictive behavior. As each member of the family wrestles with this problem, anger, blame, guilt, and depression dominate the landscape, giving more footholds for addictive acting out.

Physiological and medical problems. Many physical problems can result from food addiction. Mental function can be impaired causing everything from depression to psychosis. The heart can become weak, and the digestive system be impaired. The effects of starving can cause the kidneys to fail to operate properly; the production of blood cells is hampered, affecting the immune system and leading to anemia and weakness.

With the anorexic, the hormonal system can go out of balance causing cold intolerance, dry skin, and brittle hair. The menstrual period can stop and secondary sexual features be lost. The anorexic may also lose calcium, affecting bones and teeth.

The frequent vomiting in bulimia can inflame the esophagus, causing major problems if this continues. If laxative use is excessive, the colon can be damaged. Muscle spasms may result from low potassium levels.

We know the overweight person is more vulnerable to heart disease, hypertension, diabetes, and cancer.[12]

No more will be said about the medical characteristics of food addictions. Every addict knows his behavior is not good for him, just as a heroin addict understands the risks in substance abuse. The problem is not lack of information but finding release from the bondage of compulsion to the object or experience that produces the illusion of contentment.

SPECIFIC EATING DISORDERS

Anorexia nervosa. This is a type of food addiction characterized by preoccupation with body weight. The intense fear of becoming obese does not diminish as weight loss progresses. The anorexic has a disturbed body image so that she feels fat even when emaciated. The addict usually engages in unusual or bizarre behaviors in the handling of food. For example, she may count the number of peas she allows herself to eat. There is often refusal to eat, except for small portions, and a denial of hunger. Of course, there is a weight loss of at least twenty-five percent of the original body weight. Even though the person is dangerously under-weight, she will deny that anything is wrong. The anorexic tends to be inflexible and overcontrolled. She has an amaz-ing ability to resist the powerful hunger drive.

The anorexic often displays a high energy level and en-gages in excessive exercise. The menstrual period will usu-ally stop. As weight loss becomes severe, she develops an intolerance to cold and her hands and feet are noticeably cold. She will lose head hair but begin to grow fine body and facial hair. Constipation is common if laxative abuse takes place. Her pulse rate is slow and her blood pressure falls. At some point she will become depressed and even suicidal. Very early in the process she withdraws and be-comes alienated from family and friends.[13]

Bulimia. This form of food addiction has recurrent epi-sodes of binge eating followed by self-induced vomiting and/or purging with laxatives and/or diuretics. The addict characteristically eats high caloric, easily ingested food in a short period of time, usually less than two hours.

The symptoms include secretive binge eating, menstrual irregularities, swollen paratid (mumps) glands, cardiac ir-regularities, fluctuations of weight due to alternating binges and fasts, and a fear of the inability to stop eating voluntari-ly. The person is aware that the eating pattern is abnormal but seems unable to stop. A depressed mood and self-depre-cating thoughts follow the eating binges. The person feels guilt, shame, and despair, sometimes entertaining thoughts of suicide. Life is dominated by eating conflicts and obses-sive thoughts of food and eating. People with bulimia tend to be impulsive and undercontrolled. In contrast to the anorexic, the bulimic is unable to resist the hunger drive.

The bulimic person can maintain a seemingly normal dai-ly life of school, work, or family responsibilities. The person usually has tried many diets unsuccessfully. The secret habit can be kept concealed for years.[14]

Anorexia nervosa and bulimia. Both of these eating disorders are serious and can be life threatening. They often begin in adolescence or young adulthood, sometimes after a period of dieting or after a significant emotional trauma. Anorexia nervosa and bulimia are ten to twenty times more common among women than men. Mainly white females from middle- and upper middle-class families are affected.

The parents are usually conscientious, educated, well-meaning high achievers themselves. They are often health conscious and are careful about their diet. It is common that one or both parents tend toward perfectionism, being intolerant of mistakes in others, as well as themselves.[15]

My experience with family violence suggests that in addition to the perfectionist and over-protective family patterns, another significant contribution to the cause of eating disorders is abuse. Quite a few anorexic or bulimic females have been sexually abused. The addictive behavior is an acting out of the shame, guilt, anger, and other repressed feelings common to those who have been abused.

Some persons vacillate between the two disorders with a condition labeled bulimarexia. They rigorously diet at times and binge uncontrollably at other times. A binge is followed by fasting, laxative abuse, or other forms of purgation. Characteristics of both forms of addiction would apply.

STAGES OF FOOD ADDICTION

Food addiction, whether overeating, anorexia, or bulimia follows a pattern similar to that in all addictions.

Stage One—warning signs. This stage can start at birth. If you were born to two fat parents, you have an eighty percent chance of being fat yourself.[16] You will probably have a genetic tendency to accumulate fat cells. In addition, your fat parents are probably not going to model or instruct you in good eating habits. You are trained very early to eat too much. Now you have two strikes against you. Finally, and most important, is the use of food to relieve stress. You find that you can induce a mood alteration by eating. Rather than coping with stressors by learning new ways of adapting, you use the time-honored ritual of putting something in your mouth. And it works! Food is immediate in its effect, and is easy to obtain. No clandestine meeting in a dark alley to purchase a few grams of drugs. You just go to the cupboard and open a package of cookies.

The critical element of Stage One is immediate gratification. You want what you want, when you want it. You do not know how to delay gratification. Accompanying this is a low tolerance to stress. You don't learn how to handle stressors, you learn how to feed them. Even when you become aware of the problem, it is hard to make the necessary changes.

For those in the beginning stages of an eating disorder, what began as mild and intentional dieting becomes compulsive. Food and weight-related rituals are attempted to deal with the fear of fat. The personality begins to change and the person becomes less active in social activities. There are battles at home regarding food and exercise. The parents of the overweight person may nag about getting and staying on a diet, alternating between inducements and criticism. The family of the potential anorexic may see her as rigid, inflexible, and deviating from her overly compliant history. The addict has a low tolerance for negative feelings such as anger, grief, worry, or fear. The presence of these feelings is frequently a trigger for acting out with food.

This stage includes changes in thinking. The addict may begin to resent thin or normal people, and may feel in competition with them for grades, popularity, work assignments, affection, and attention. Having learned to deal with stress by eating, the food addict begins to displace many of his fears and concerns onto weight. He has irrational beliefs about food and weight. "If I eat that sandwich I will gain back five pounds almost instantly." "I can't do anything about my weight. Nothing will work." "I am a disgusting person, and nobody will love me if I continue to eat the way I am now." These are examples of the type of thinking that can occur at this stage.

Stage Two—out-of-control obsessions. At this stage the addiction becomes dominant. The attraction to food is employed to escape worries and to avoid dealing with issues such as schoolwork, employment challenges, marital conflicts, or management of children.

A lifestyle of food abuse has been established, so the addict has to give increasing attention to maintaining sufficient supplies for the "fix." Excessive amounts of time are spent thinking about food, shopping for food, cooking food, or eating out. One extreme or the other is present—either the addict avoids any discussion about food and weight or constantly talks about them.

The addict is constantly planning for a diet, is on a diet, or is in between diets. Periods of fasting, binging, or constant overeating predominate. He secretly eats in public, while shopping or driving for example. In anticipation of periods when food might not be available, the addict will overeat to avoid getting hungry. There are strong compulsions to eat even though he just ate.

He is embarrassed about the amounts he eats, so he makes more excuses to eat in private. He doesn't want to appear hungry in public so eats at home before going out to dinner. He gets in the habit of gulping down food before being discovered. He even eats when he doesn't feel like it. His secret life has now fully developed. He knows he is out of control and feels guilty, but uses food to make the bad feelings go away.

Denial is rampant. The addict denies there is weight gain, or else says, "It's not really that much." There is a shutting out of the cause-and-effect relationship between the empty ice cream carton and body fat. While eating, the addict blocks out the consequences of his behavior. He tells himself, "It's okay. I'll start my diet tomorrow and get rid of everything I've gained." Eventually, emotional fatigue sets in and he gives up hope of ever being in control.[17]

If it hasn't already taken place, at this time the person begins to doubt God. He has undoubtedly prayed that God would help him regain control. The prayers seem not to have been answered so a fatalistic, spiritual emptiness begins to form. God is left out of conscious thinking. Church, Bible study, fellowship groups, etc. are often dropped to avoid being reminded of his spiritual failure.

With the anorexic, this stage is characterized by significant weight loss, and nutritional deprivation. The person is committed to anorexic ways of thinking and acting. The preoccupation with food, food-related rituals, exercise, and denial of problems is monumental. Most of the symptoms described earlier are fully present. The condition is acute and receptivity to treatment may be very poor.

Stage Three—entrenched compulsion. The addiction becomes all-consuming. The addict eats until nauseated, even though it no longer produces the elevated mood change and demand. She is unable to cope with any but minimal or survival tasks. Withdrawal symptoms are experienced in brief efforts to exert willpower. Feelings of hopelessness and futility are overwhelming. Nothing matters but food. It doesn't make her feel any better, but the habit is entrenched so deep the behavior pattern continues. Elaborate alibis and justifications are made for the eating patterns. "I have a hormonal imbalance," or "A food allergy makes me eat this way."

Blaming and projection become common. Food doesn't

produce the fix it used to. She still feels depressed and guilty. Family members, society, classmates, coworkers, etc. are blamed for all her problems. "Who wouldn't eat themselves to death if they had to live in a place like this?"

By this time, the behavior pattern of overeating, anorexia, or bulimia has become well established. It may have gone on for years. The habit has become intrinsic to the personality. The addict sees the world primarily through the eyes of an eating disorder and is unable to handle intimate contact with others. There is total inability to cope without food rituals and obsessions.

In the case of anorexia and bulimia, hospitalization may be required. The weight loss, nutritional deficiencies, medical problems, and family chaos usually combine to force a drastic form of intervention. There are often life-threatening symptoms that require immediate medical attention. The first order of business is to get the person medically stabilized and then begin to work out the emotional, intellectual, spiritual, and social problems.

Spiritual awareness is almost completely dead at this stage. The addict knows she is totally out of control. God has abandoned her and she is cynical. She has no hope and, furthermore, she doesn't care.

SELF-EVALUATION
The following questions will help you determine if you have an addiction to food. Answer each question honestly. Remember, you can't start your recovery until you admit your condition.

TEST FOR FOOD ADDICTION

_____ 1. Are you either twenty percent over or under your ideal body weight for your age and build?

_____ 2. Have you made many desperate attempts to lose weight by going on fad diets, fasting, using pills, buying weight loss equipment, or taking classes?

_____ 3. Do you find yourself thinking about your weight or food several times through a normal day?

_____ 4. Have you had any health problems related to your weight or eating habits?

_____ 5. Do you struggle with feelings of low self-esteem because of your weight or eating habits?

_____ 6. Do you often think about having enough food, where you will get it, or how to prepare it?

_____ 7. Do you eat when you are depressed, anxious, angry?

_____ 8. Does food make you feel better?

_____ 9. Do you find relationships with people to be difficult?

_____ 10. Are you a perfectionist? Do you have high expectations for yourself, but struggle with not meeting your goals?

_____ 11. Have you found that the ability to make yourself feel better by either eating or losing weight gives you a sense of control or power?

_____ 12. Have you experienced confusion about your identity as a man or woman?

_____ 13. Do you struggle with depression, or feelings of guilt and shame?

_____ 14. Have you lied, deceived, or attempted to hide your eating behavior from family or friends?

_____ 15. Have you found yourself resenting thin people?

_____ 16. Do you sometimes binge and then fast, make yourself throw up, use laxatives or diuretics to lose weight?

_____ 17. Do you feel compelled to eat, or not to eat, at certain times?

_____ 18. Have you eaten to the point of hurting, getting sick, or passing out?

_____ 19. Do you feel out of control in regard to your eating habits?

_____ 20. Do you feel hopeless, discouraged, or have even thought about suicide, as a result of your relationship with food?

If you answered yes to three or more of the questions, you may well have a food addiction. Because of the specific nature of the questions, if you gave a positive response to any of them, you should evaluate your relationship to food.

WHAT TO DO?

Most Americans have struggled with food. For the addict it isn't just a struggle but an overwhelming, overpowering, ever present obsession with food. It controls your entire life. There is no peace or place of contentment. It is constant misery. But what do you do about it? Chances are you have read dozens of books about the subject and none of them provided the cure.

I don't want to add to your pain by giving you false hope.

I'm not proposing ten easy steps to recovery and peace of mind, because I know it is hard and painful. But I have to believe that God intends for us to be healthy and free from compulsive behavior (John 8:32; 10:10). My contribution, then, is to try to share my integration of the spiritual components of recovery with the best understanding of the psychological aspects of the road to a balanced life.

Get help. If you have several of the symptoms of anorexia nervosa or bulimia, I suggest you immediately make an appointment with a Christian psychologist, psychiatrist, or other qualified mental health professional. Make sure it is someone who is experienced in working with eating disorders. Get suggestions from your doctor, pastor, or from family or friends. You could also contact one of the organizations listed in the resource section of this book. They may be able to give you a contact person in your region.

Regardless of the type of addiction, professional help is advised. If your situation has reached the latter parts of the second stage or into the third stage, it may be life-threatening and may need immediate medical intervention to stabilize your body. At the very least, your body will need to go through some form of detoxification. You will need a qualified medical team to help you do this. Remember, when you look for help, you're not asking for a simple diet or weight loss program. You need instruction on how to live differently. Following any necessary medical help, the reeducation can begin. Prepare yourself to spend one to two years in this intense stage of recovery. You have many issues to cover, and the process can't be rushed. You must learn to deal with perfectionism, low self-esteem, your sexual identity, deception, struggles for power in your family, interdependency with family members, and any physical or medical complications that have come out of your abuse of food.

Group support. Either as an initial step or as a supplement to therapy, a Twelve Step group such as Overeaters Anonymous is recommended. There are many reasons for this, the most important of which is that it works! Recovery from food addiction means turning away from the self-administered comfort of food and learning instead how to receive nurturance from people. A support group like Overeaters Anonymous can help you do this.

Scripture tells us that "every matter must be established by two or three witnesses" (2 Corinthians 13:1). While this specific reference is referring back to Old Testament legal procedures, I think we can also make the principle apply to the use of groups. In a group setting, you can share your experience and by that sharing, be guided toward truth by feedback from the group.

Take recovery seriously. The addiction to food is probably a lifetime condition. However, the condition can be managed. You have developed an unhealthy attachment to food, partly as a result of not being able to form appropriate relationships. You will have to learn how to give up your love affair with food and learn how to love and be loved by people. This is risky business. Food was a reliable fix; people are not. Food was always there to provide nurturance; people may fail you.

Many food addicts believe that if they could just learn to eat normally and maintain their ideal body weight, everything would be fine. There's more to it than that. Recovery is more than counting calories. It is learning a new lifestyle. You must develop a positive way of dealing with the stressors of everyday living so that you don't need to escape into food to survive.

If you desire to lose weight permanently while remaining healthy and productive, you must take a serious inventory of yourself. You need to become a convert to "thin-thinking" and be prepared for a degree of persistent discomfort from your relentless commitment to recovery.

Making the commitment to recovery means you will have to constantly remind yourself how serious your addiction is. You have spent a lifetime being powerless over food. That fact must be accepted, but it doesn't end there. The truth of your chronic addiction must be considered in all matters at all times. You can't put it on the back burner and forget it when things are going okay. You must now make recovery permeate your life as much as food did before.[18]

You need to recognize that if you are overweight, it is because you eat too much and exercise too little. Crash dieting should be ruled out; it almost always results in failure and lowered self-esteem. The best diets involve losing no more than one pound a week. This means it will take a long time to do; it happens with healthy eating, a reasonable intake of calories, an increased amount of exercise, and a program of changing your habits of when, where, and how you eat. It's got to be slow and long to last for a lifetime.[19]

Accept God's help. Time and again we have highlighted the necessity of acknowledging your powerlessness over food. Willpower is not enough. You must surrender your efforts to the wisdom and power of God. This becomes a matter of faith (Ephesians 2:8). If you are struggling with food or any other type of addiction, you must believe that Jesus Christ died on the cross for your sins (John 3:16; Romans 6:23). He died to take away your sins and give eternal life to those who make a personal decision to believe in Him (Acts 2:21). You have been given the promise of a transformed life (John 5:24; 2 Corinthians 5:17). God offers His grace to enable you to develop a new mind, a new way of thinking, and a new way of behaving (Romans 12:2; 2 Corinthians 4:16; Colossians 3:10).

This power from God provides the ability to develop a new lifestyle free from compulsive behavior and from the misbeliefs that energized it all. For example, the misbelief might be, "I can't lose weight or control my eating habits." There are differences in fat cells from one person to another. Some people, indeed, have a predisposition to be obese. But the primary reason people are overweight is that they overeat and underexercise. As we have seen, there are many reasons addicts overeat, but it is their overeating that causes the problem.

The belief must be changed to, "I can learn to eat and exercise in ways that are under control and healthy because I can do all things through Christ who strengthens me" (see Philippians 4:13). First the belief system must be changed; then the compulsive behavior will change.

Change your belief system. This is an important part of your recovery. Your counselor and support group will spend a great deal of time on self-defeating and faulty ways of thinking.

Our thinking often includes irrational assumptions which are based on the idea that "things are done to us." A better way of thinking is to say that "certain things happen in the world." An event such as a child's temper tantrum may influence your behavior, but it was not done "to you."

A way of viewing the development of our responses to situations is to say there are three components: A—you experience an event, B—You engage in self-talk about the event, and C—You experience an emotion.

The event (A) does not cause your emotion (C). Rather, what you tell yourself (B) causes your emotions. For example, if your husband criticizes the condition of the house (A), you might tell yourself (B) "I never do anything right. I am a failure, just like my father told me I would be." The result (C) might be feelings of depression, discouragement, and resentment.

If your self-talk is irrational and unrealistic, you are likely to experience unpleasant emotions. This does not mean that by achieving some ideal level of "perfect" self-talk you will eliminate all negative feelings. That is not the goal. Many uncomfortable feelings are normal and useful. To grieve over the death of a loved one, for example, is an appropriate reaction. The goal is to first be aware of the connection between your internal statements and your feelings, and second, to lessen the number of unrealistic or irrational statements.

There are two common forms of irrational self-talk found in food addicts. There are statements that *awfulize*. For example, "I can't stand being alone." "I'll die if he doesn't call." or "I must have gained ten pounds from that dessert."

Second are irrational self-statements that *absolutize*. For example, "Since I ate dessert, I don't have any self-control," or "No one will like me if I don't lose weight."[20]

It may be helpful at this point to write out some of your beliefs about food, weight, self-control, God, and other related topics. Don't edit them or try to change them for the better; just get them down on paper so you can examine them.

Take several days to complete this task. Be as thorough as possible. Then go back over your statements and evaluate the truthfulness of each one. You have a web of beliefs and thoughts to untangle, so you may well need the help of a counselor and/or support group to make much progress.

Regain control of your eating habits. Once you have stabilized your body, established a relationship with a counselor and/or support group, you can begin a program to manage your relationship with food. There are lots of food management programs available. I will briefly list some elements which should be helpful. Your own treatment team will be able to tailor a program that meets your nutritional and emotional needs. Here are some suggestions.

• Plan your meals and snacks. Eat three meals per day with

snacks as needed. Do not skip breakfast. Going too long without food sets you up to overeat.

- Eat a portion from each of the major food groups each day: milk, meat, fruits/vegetables, and grains. The different food groups break down at different rates. Therefore, it is helpful to eat from at least two or three groups at each meal.
- Make a shopping list from your meal plan. Buy appropriate quantities to meet your food management goals. No impulse buying. If it's not on your list, wait until next time.
- Sit at a table to eat. Avoid eating in front of the TV, in the bedroom, in the car, etc.
- Do not engage in other activities when eating, such as reading, watching TV, doing paperwork, etc.
- Avoid all or nothing thinking. Binge eating may be related to irrational beliefs such as, "I've already blown it by eating one cookie, so I might as well eat the whole bag!" or, "I'm never going to eat cake again, so I might as well finish the whole thing and get it out of the way."
- Your optimal weight is the weight at which you have the most energy and feel your best physically. Your body has a "set point" and can be trusted to self-regulate if you increase your awareness of when you are physically hungry or full. Eat according to your physical hunger and exercise moderately.
- If you have food phobias or forbidden foods, begin to plan them into your menu in small amounts.
- If you believe you have food allergies that exacerbate food management problems, or if specific foods appear to cause a physiological craving, you should consult a physician or nutritionist.
- To gain or lose weight, do not cut out whole groups of foods. Instead, cut or add portions of foods.
- Weight alone is not a good indicator of losing fat. Weight can reflect a change in muscle mass, body water, or body fat content. Scales cannot discriminate between big bones, well-developed muscles, excess water retention, or too much fat. Therefore, use some form of *body composition* testing. This can be done easily by using a portable instrument that measures electrical impedance.[21]

To establish obesity, it is necessary to measure the amount of body fat and compare it to some standard of acceptable fatness in a specified population. Sex, age, and physical activity must be considered. It is a reasonable guideline to call males obese if their body fat is in excess of twenty percent of their total body weight. For females the guideline would be twenty-eight percent.[22]

- Eat refined sugar or other sweets with your meal rather than by themselves. This avoids wide blood sugar fluctuations which may result in fatigue, depression, or cravings.

- Relax through meditation, prayer, or deep breathing before you begin to eat.

- Eat slowly. Focus on the food. Savor it. This will promote satiety, aid digestion, and give your stomach time to get the message to your brain when you begin to be full.

- Take individual portions each time you want food. Do not eat out of the serving dish or container.

- In order to develop internal control (eating when hungry rather than eating everything in sight), you can practice cutting portions and getting in the habit of leaving a portion of food on your plate after a meal. If you need to gain, rather than lose or maintain weight, add portions.

- Keep a food log. This will help you begin to identify patterns of food management. Increased awareness allows you to make good choices.

- Eat at planned meal and snack times. When you begin to feel satisfied (full), stop eating. If it is difficult to stop eating or to eat as much as your body needs, analyze why that is so.

- If you overeat, be flexible, forgive yourself, and figure out how to "minimize the damage"—by cutting back at the next meal, waiting longer than usual to eat again, exercising more, etc. Do not punish yourself. That only leads to more negative feelings and increased overeating.

- Moderate exercise will burn excess calories, increase your metabolism, improve muscle tone, and help you avoid depression.[23]

Involve your family. As you move through your recovery, things will change. Your family has become very used to your addictive behavior. Some of them may even have become codependent, and will need to learn how to detach from the unhealthy aspect of their relationship. As you change, your family will need to change. This is a complicated issue. I would suggest *Fat Is a Family Affair* by Judi Hollis. Your counselor or support group will have additional suggestions.

Yes, there is life without a compulsive relationship to food. In its place are new sensations, new feelings, new risks, and even new fears. But there is also new hope and new faith. What was once unmanageable can now be handled one day at a time. Concentrate on today. With God's help you can make it to a place of serenity. May God bless.

N O T E S

1. Judi Hollis, *Fat Is a Family Affair* (San Francisco: Hazelden), 1985, 19.
2. Mike Nelson, "Shattered Lives: The Agony of Eating Disorders," *Valley Magazine*, March 1986.
3. M. Simonson, "Obesity as a Health Factor," *Female Patient*, 1978, 85–87.
4. G.L. Blackburn, "Pathophysiology and Metabolism," in *Obesity*, G.L. Blackburn, ed. (Boston Center for Nutritional Research), 1977, 1–22.
5. D.M. Vickery and J.F. Fries, *Taking Care of Yourself: A Consumer's Guide to Medical Care* (Reading, Addison-Wesley), 1976.
6. Sandra Haber, "Obesity: The Psychology of a Multifaceted Volitional Disorder," in *Behavior in Excess*, S. Joseph Mule, ed. (New York: The Free Press), 1981, 211–212.
7. Nelson, "Shattered Lives: The Agony of Eating Disorders."
8. Hollis, *Fat Is a Family Affair*, 8.
9. Raymond Vath, *Counseling Those with Eating Disorders* (Dallas: Word Books), 1986, 31–32.
10. *Ibid.*, 146.
11. *Ibid.*, 153–154.
12. *Ibid.*, 39–58.
13. *Ibid.*, 36–37.
14. *Ibid.*, 37.
15. *Ibid.*, 37–38.
16. Hollis, *Fat Is a Family Affair*, 34.
17. *Ibid.*, 35–36.
18. *Ibid.*, 79.
19. Harvey Milkman and Stanley Sunderwirth, *Craving for Ecstasy: The Consciousness & Chemistry of Escape*, (Lexington, Mississippi: D.C. Heath) 1987, 87.
20. Cheryl Merrill, "Understanding and Treating Eating Disorders: A Christian Perspective," presented at Christian Association for Psychological Studies, Denver, 1988.
21. Henry Lukaski, Phyllis Johnson, William Bolonchuk, and Glenn Lykken. "Assessment of fat-free mass using bioelectrical impedance measurements of the human body," *The American Journal of Clinical Nutrition*, 41. April 1985, 810–817.
22. Gordon G. Ball and Joel A. Grinker, "Overeating and Obesity," in *Behavior in Excess*, S. Joseph Mule, ed. (New York: The Free Press), 1981, 194.
23. Cheryl Merrill, "Understanding and Treating Eating Disorders: A Christian Perspective."

POWER ADDICTION
Do You Need to Be in Control?

● Fred entered the counselor's office loaded for bear. Fred's wife, Sally, had been talking to this counselor for several weeks, and Fred didn't like the outcome. He was going to show the counselor, from the Word of God, how his wife was destroying the family by refusing to come home.

Sally started seeing the counselor after informing Fred she would not take the abuse and his domineering attitude anymore. She then moved out and obtained an order of protection to keep Fred from harassing her further. Fred was furious that she would go public about private family problems and that she would defy his authority as head of the household. His own pastor was supportive of Sally, but after seeking out several other pastors, Fred was convinced his wife had a rebellious spirit. With this perspective in mind, Fred was going to prove his position to the counselor if it took all afternoon.

Fred had worked at several careers and was now self-employed selling real estate. He had built a beautiful home overlooking the golf course where he spent several afternoons a week with friends and clients. There were two BMWs in the garage, and a sports car for their son, along with a thirty-foot cruiser moored down at the lake. Fred had the biggest and best of everything, but always kept the finances under his exclusive control. He attended church irregularly until Sally left. After that he went to three churches several times a week telling everybody who would listen how his wife had deserted the family and rejected everything he had done for her.

Sally's story was quite different. She was only nineteen when she married. Fred had just been discharged from the service and had big plans for their lives. He seldom asked about her feelings or wishes; he made plans and implemented them, usually telling her what was going on at the last minute. Over the past five years there had been an increasing number of intense physical outbursts. Fred had actually hit her several times, and would often be verbally abusive. He would then blame Sally for causing him to lose control. Later, Fred would apologize, but these eruptions seemed to be more intense and frequent.

Power, prestige, honor, acclaim, status, control, and influence—pretty compelling terms. If you think drugs or sex can make you feel good, try pulling off a two million dollar sale, masterminding the takeover of a profitable company, or being named the outstanding performer in your field. There's nothing like it. And it's perfectly legal.

Power addiction is the progressive desire to be more than we are; it leads to destruction and disunity. Achieving and maintaining power is the attempt to give meaning to life by the use of influence and some form of manipulation or control of relationships. Generally, power is equated with influence, money, and position. While we would like to think otherwise, Christians are as vulnerable to the addictive use of power as they are to sex or food. An addiction is progressive, harmful, and seductive. Power meets the criteria on all three counts.

FUNCTION OF POWER ADDICTION

Pastor Stan was a fine preacher. In fact, some would have put him in the orator class. People came by the hundreds to hear him preach in what started out as a small independent church near a large city. After a couple of years, Pastor Stan was asked to do a local TV show, and his reputation widened. Confident that his people were behind him, Pastor Stan took on some community leaders over their resistance to building desperately needed low income housing projects. The issue was passed and several more projects achieved similar results. God seemed to be using Pastor Stan in rather remarkable and practical ways.

Gradually, however, some internal changes took place which later led to disaster. With the support of the elders, Pastor Stan was given CEO authority in the church government. The previous system of checks and balances was replaced by singular responsibility for the senior pastor. A building program was initiated, and when a crucial deadline drew near, the pastor asked everybody to sign statements of allegiance and commit to a fixed financial pledge. When the building proved to be more expensive than anticipated, the pastor, without consulting the elders, asked each family to increase their pledge by seven percent. Later, the elders discovered that numerous unauthorized changes to the building had been implemented by the pastor, accounting for a large portion of the overrun.

Being an independent church, there was no denominational accountability or responsibility. The pastor resisted suggestions to join an association of independent churches, saying such an affiliation was a waste of time and money. Several youth ministers were called, but they only lasted six months or so. Each time Pastor Stan blamed the problems on their lack of experience and unwillingness to submit to his authority.

His sermons began to take on a dogmatic, intolerant tone. He increasingly castigated any point of view that deviated from his interpretation. Anyone who disagreed was described as a "tool of the devil." Public tongue-lashings of named individuals took place regularly. Elders who raised questions were ridiculed in his sermons. A few members who had been there from the beginning knew something had gone wrong, but they didn't know what to do about it. Finally, things came crashing down when several women in the church reported sexual involvement with Pastor Stan, and a long overdue audit of the books revealed large sums of money were missing. Another leader had fallen.

We have learned that addictive experiences serve several functions. They can help us make up for weaknesses, avoid intimacy, shut out pain, provide a sense of control, or make us feel good. Power can do all of these things, and others, rather well. Let's look at each of these. The pastor described above will make a good case study.

Compensation. Stan had always been a good student growing up, but seldom made close friends. His family moved frequently as his father achieved progressive promotions. Whenever Stan would complain, his parents would drive home the fact of education being the most important part of his life. Stan was told he could always make friends, but he dare not miss out on his schooling.

Stan was teased some about his big ears and glasses. Never good in sports, he learned to compensate for his lack of social status by being a good student and imitating TV preachers in the privacy of his room. This pattern of compensation continued as a young adult. A youth pastor encouraged him to go into the ministry, so Stan went to a Bible college and then to seminary. Along the way he entered into student government and found satisfaction in being a leader and rallying behind causes and issues. Stan never really bonded with his classmates, but found a great deal of satisfaction in "being in charge."

Stan's use of power to gain status helped him compensate for other deficiencies. He wasn't very good at making friends, but he knew how to win an election. The same function is true for all power abusers; it may be an attempt to make up for low self-esteem. Many an addict has spent his or her entire life trying to achieve success to make up for earlier failures or weaknesses. The fallacy is that performance alone cannot give a person a sense of being or self-esteem. Since power does not answer the core question, "Who am I?" the addict pursues the carrot with even more intensity, perpetuating the cycle.

Avoidance of intimacy. Following the pattern of his youth, Stan learned to use activity, issues, rhetoric, and control as ways to avoid intimacy. He did not have the emotional experience to relate at deeper levels with his peers. In his church, the pulpit was his wall of protection. If somebody tried to get too close, Stan would use his position to maintain a comfortable distance. Yes, he was an attractive personality. His public image was quite desirable so that people were drawn by the aura of his confident manner. Whenever someone, such as an elder, made an effort to draw out his feelings, Stan would change the subject, intellectualize, or even get angry. For years, everyone who saw this would excuse the pastor because "he was working under a lot of stress," or "he couldn't be expected to be both a people person and a pulpit person."

As long as things went his way, Pastor Stan could afford to be rigid and unyielding. Intimacy wasn't necessary. Things worked well without his having to take the risk of being vulnerable. But the seductive nature of power began to show itself as the pastor took more liberties. Unconsciously,

Stan began to think he was invincible, immune from the power of temptation. There was no mentor, no honest prayer partner who would love Stan unconditionally, but also hold him accountable for his decisions. Stan fell to the seductive influence of power because he was afraid to disclose his humanness.

Elimination of pain. A prospective client called and told me he needed an appointment to fulfill the requirements of a court order. It seems he had been physically abusive to his family; he was arrested and told he wouldn't have to go to jail if he could show he had satisfactorily completed an anger management course. As we talked, he revealed a sad and traumatic childhood. There were numerous emotional losses and extensive physical and sexual abuse. None of that had ever been reported. He never got help, and the memories never left him. This six-foot five-inch mountain of a man contained a scared, hurt little boy. On the outside there was an aggressive, intimidating man who always took control of a situation. On the inside was a mountain of pain weeping for consolation and relief. His use of power served to numb the pain, but the source never went away.

Pastor Stan used control, manipulation, and position to avoid his pain. The more he progressed into the addiction, the more shame, guilt, and agony he experienced. As the anguish increased, he resorted to higher levels of control to try to ease the pain. He became more dogmatic, and placed greater expectations on his congregation and family. He eliminated the elders from parts of crucial decision-making. It was taking higher and higher levels of acting out to subdue the pain. Disaster is imminent under these conditions.

Control. This is the "magic wand" dimension of power. By waving the scepter, the addict makes changes in her world. By her command people respond. By her decree programs are implemented. People seek the information or resources that she holds. The earth is a different place as a result of her action. They make a wish, rub her brass Aladdin's lamp, and their request is granted. Power offers this kind of potential.

For the power addict, the ability to affect a mood change is brought about by seeing people and situations respond to his initiative and leadership. This gives the addict an identity. It feeds the selfish child within who learned as an infant to control the environment by crying, cooing, or grimacing.

We all have a very basic need to understand the world around us. This began with Adam and Eve. Richard Foster makes the following observation:

> *Think of Adam and Eve in the garden—given every pleasure, every delight, everything necessary for a good life. Yet they wanted more; they grasped and grabbed in a headlong rush to be like God, to know good and evil. The sin of the garden was the sin of power. They wanted to be more, to have more, to know more than is right. Not content to be creatures, they wanted to be gods.* [1]

The legacy of Adam and Eve exerts its influence on each of us so that we are not content to live at peace with our world. We feel drawn to achieve predominance. We want to own, accumulate, and conquer. We are not satisfied with our created existence but want to be gods. Not only does this fragment our relationships to fellow humans, but it separates us from God. We are too busy trying to establish our own type of dominion to hear His voice.

Pastor Stan grew deaf to God as his addiction to power grew. His initial good intentions were corrupted by the euphoric effects of people and situations responding to his control. God's power working through us restores relationships, sets people free, and produces unity. Unfortunately, Stan's actions, like all power addicts, fragmented relationships, put people in bondage, and created disunity.

Identity. Power and all its functions give us a name. With power we have an identity. Remember the disciples arguing over who would be the "greatest" in the kingdom of God? (Luke 9:46; 22:24) They were concerned about who would be "first" or "last." Rank was important, even to the followers of Jesus. They were concerned more about their designation than about their functioning as instruments of God. In other words, the apostles were worrying more about the label on their tunics, than about how the fabric would hold up in the hot Samaritan air and sand.

They had been taught about true greatness when Jesus instructed them to be servants, just as He had modeled (Luke 22:27). Yet, this message had not yet taken root in their understanding and inner being. They had heard Jesus teach that their identity lay not in treasures of this earth

(Matthew 6:19; Luke 12:21) or in their community status (Luke 18:9-14). But the old nature still wanted to be king of the hill.

Pastor Stan found his identity wrapped up in being a champion of community issues, friend of the homeless, a great preacher, and leader of a growing church. These labels gave him the illusion of personhood. As long as the designation fit, he had meaning. The addiction, however, demanded more and more labels. Just being a good pulpit preacher was no longer enough to obtain the fix needed to make Stan feel good. Absent was an enduring sense of being a servant of God through which God channeled His power. In the end, Stan believed it was his singular responsibility to keep everything together. And it proved to be an impossible task.

Perks. How do you think it feels to be chauffered up to the front door of your own office building and then escorted inside with the admiring looks and comments of knowledgeable bystanders and employees? You ride the elevator to the top of the building where the executive suites are perched overlooking the bay and the mountains. There is fine wood paneling on the walls, thick carpet, fine furnishings, soft music, and well-tailored assistants everywhere you turn.

As the day progresses, telephones, fax machines, and computers provide information about the expanding and profitable nature of your business. You make decisions that affect the lives of thousands of people. Admirers are constantly complimenting your ability and business acumen.

At the end of the day, you walk up to the rooftop of your building. A waiting helicopter takes you to a hotel across town where you are to address a banquet of prestigious leaders in your industry. The group gives you a standing ovation and an award as the outstanding businessperson in America. Pretty heady stuff, right? Power makes you feel good.

Status, authority, prestige, and adulation are certain to create a mood-altering experience. The brain undergoes chemical changes similar to ingesting a mind-altering drug. The drug, sex, and food addicts have in common with the power addict that it feels good. The body learns to crave the change in feelings that come with the mood-altering experience. The feelings associated with power take on a life and meaning of their own. Pretty soon it's not the activities of power that are needed, but the feelings that come with being seen as powerful.

In our case study, Pastor Stan struggled with feelings of guilt, shame, and depression. When he heard his TV audience applaud, his negative feelings took a temporary turn for the better. He was accepted. His position of power created situations that helped him feel good.

The example of the power-abusing husband was not as public in nature. There was no audience rising in appreciation, no awards, and no building with his name on it. Rather, the mood-altering experiences were private. But there is no doubt that for an addict, having the last word with a spouse, seeing her comply to his demands, and being seen by family as the exclusive authority in the home, is every bit as seductive.

Organization of chaos. The final function of power addiction is its ability to make order out of disorder. Life is unpredictable. People do not always do what we expect. Circumstances get out of hand. All of this creates frustration. It may be as minor as a shoestring breaking while we're rushing to get ready for church, or as major as a child dropping out of school.

A power-abusive spouse or parent will often be motivated to overcontrol her environment to keep order. By demanding, making threats, issuing ultimatums, offering inducements, or withdrawing favors, the power addict makes her world more predictable. Being able to predetermine one's future would give any of us a sense of control. Our reality requires, however, that we learn to tolerate some degree of ambiguity and indecision. One of the marks of maturity is to be able to handle a lack of certainty. Trust and faith also mean that we place our hope on an omnipotent God, not in our own understanding (Proverbs 3:5-6). Our paths are not made straight by our own insight or manipulation, but by the providence of God. That doesn't mean we stand by helplessly wringing our hands, wondering what will happen next. It calls for a balance between exercising appropriate faith in God, and using the wisdom that He gives to us.

The addict does not have this balance. Power serves as a tool to make the world as predictable as possible. The elimination of chaos brings about a change in mood. Instead of panic and anxiety, there is peace and calm. The acting out is reinforced by the alteration of the mood. Suppose a harried mother of three spends the first five hours of her day doing laundry, answering phone calls, preparing meals, arbitrating arguments, cleaning house, and chasing dogs out of the flower beds. Finally, in an act of desperation, she issues a parental ultimatum, "Go to your rooms, take a nap, and don't let me hear a word out of any of you for at least an hour!"

In the ensuing minutes, Mom sits down for the first time all day with a cup of tea and soaks in the sounds of silence. Her exercise of authority has gained her a short respite from the hassles of normal routine. Her power has created order out of chaos. In this case, it is legitimate; but the same principle can lead to addiction when allowed to continue unchecked. Suppose six months later, after countless frustrations, lack of support by her husband, and financial pressures, our mother is using her adult power to scream and to beat the children into compliance. Each episode gives her a few minutes of peace. However, the progressive nature of addiction is evident. It now takes more intense forms of control to obtain even a small change in mood. Unwittingly, she has become entrapped to the immediate effects of power to create order.

Pastor Stan began to experience a deterioration in his church and community. A building program seldom goes according to plans since there are countless unanticipated problems. This was true for Pastor Stan. Finances began to get out of control, so he exerted his power to attempt to create order again. This cycle of imbalance and rebalancing extracted a heavy toll on Stan. His attachment to power was enhanced by his increasing need to organize chaos.

CHARACTERISTICS OF POWER ADDICTION

There are many signs and symptoms of addiction to power. We will not discuss again the characteristics of all addictions, which include denial, immediacy, compulsion, loss of control, progression, and withdrawal. However, there are some characteristics more unique to an attachment to power and control.

Prejudice. Most people have opinions about certain things. The power addict is strongly opinionated about almost everything. She is quite biased and prejudiced about how things should be done and how life should be lived. In the home, the power addict gives directives about schedules, procedures, values, and choices. Very little escapes review. Even when the addict has no experience or training, she has opinions. Family gatherings are painful, because she takes every opportunity to voice how she feels about most every topic that presents itself.

Consistency is supposed to be a virtue. In this case, it means the addict never lets up. Wherever she goes, the opinions follow. If people have a choice, they will tend to avoid the power addict, because the discussions never get anywhere. The addict has all the facts she needs. The best rule for others to follow is "Save time, do it my way."

Inflexibility. Besides having strong opinions and biases, the power addict is arbitrary and inflexible. He seems unable to compromise, when concession would be appropriate. His thinking tends to be all or nothing, rigid and unforgiving. "Red-necked" might be an appropriate label for many power addicts, although the content should not be limited to political beliefs. An inflexible power addict can be as arbitrary about liberal values as others can be about conservative beliefs.

This type of addict also has trouble laughing off mistakes or looking at the humorous side of his humanness. It may be funny when somebody else makes a mistake, but it is no laughing matter when he commits a faux pas.

Problems with anger. Many power addicts have tempers that are easily triggered. Some may be verbally or emotionally abusive, while others may be physically abusive. Their language will include a great deal of sarcasm, and their humor tends to be degrading. They may laugh all right, but often at the expense of others.

There are two possible patterns of anger control. The first is explosive outrage. The individual gets angry at his wife because she didn't enter a check in the register. He shouts, chews her out, maybe even gets insulting. There's no question about his being angry and why.

The second pattern is much more passive, but just as much a form of control. The person lets things build up inside for days or weeks. She doesn't say much about her frustrations until one little thing blows the cork off of the bottle. Then all of the incidents and resentments of the past weeks are paraded out and dumped at the feet of the offending victim.

A variation of this second pattern is the person who really never blows up. There is very little expression of visible anger, but it does show up in passive aggressive behavior. The person may not complete assigned tasks, may agree to show up for something but doesn't make it or comes late. The pattern is a type of stubborn refusal to cooperate because he is resentful about previous violations of his expectations.

"Nit-picking." Here the addict is demanding and hard to please. She picks at flaws and is never satisfied with the final product. The child never mows the lawn neatly enough. The husband doesn't earn enough money or spend enough time with the children, even though he has improved in both regards.

The bottom line is that the perfectionist expectations are never met, regardless of how hard the other person tries or how high he jumps. The addict is continually complaining that "other people don't know what they are doing." There are lots of "If only. . . " statements such as, "If only they would let me do it my way, they wouldn't be having so many problems."

There are certainly problems in life. Nobody does everything right. But for the power addict, the focus on failure is continual and intense. It's as if he has to put the efforts of others down in order to overcome his own sense of failure.

Double standard. Many power addicts hold a double standard for behavior. They can use foul language, but their children dare not utter a profane word or they will catch it. Some may require their employees to put in long hours and diligent effort while they take off at noon to play golf, leaving their responsibilities to secretaries who are underpaid and undervalued.

There is a lot of denial, as the addict makes excuses for himself, but seldom allows others the same opportunity. It is hard for the power addict to admit failure. He hates like everything to say he is sorry, and seldom does.

If someone were to bring up any of these traits we are talking about here, the addict would deny their application to her. Or she would make excuses for her behavior, saying something like, "I've been under a lot of stress lately, and I just haven't been myself."

Manipulation. It goes without saying that the power addict has to get his own way. Otherwise, there is no control. The whole process is nourished by the addictive nature of success. The power addict gets hooked because he has found ways to avoid pain, escape intimacy, or feel good by manipulating others.

There are two general styles in which this can be done. One is the roaring lion; the other is the sneaky fox. The *roaring lion* gets his way by intimidation and confrontation. If things aren't going according to specifications, the offending person is called on the carpet in no uncertain terms. The roaring lion has many tools. Verbal confrontations such as harassment, persuasion, threats, or warnings can be used. The lion likes to dominate. His line is something like, "I'm the boss around here, and you do as I say or get out."

The *sneaky fox,* as you might guess, is more subtle. His tools are more crafty, cunning, and calculating than confrontive. The fox may make promises to get a commitment from you, and then fail to make good on her promise. The fox is more likely to use compliments, flattery, false promises, and deceit to get what she wants. Within a family, the fox will enlist other family members to put pressure on someone to change his mind. She might also use guilt induction or shaming tactics to motivate a child or spouse to do what she desires.

Both forms of manipulation can work. And because they work, there will always be addicts who become enslaved to their enticing enchantment.

Pious power. Resorting to piety is a power play unique to Christians. It is a particularly insidious form of manipulation. It works quite well, but leaves a very bad aftertaste. For Christians, the more spiritual one is, the more powerful.[2]

Spirituality brings followers. The more followers you have, it is assumed, the more spiritual you must be. Pastor Stan was caught up in this belief, and it eventually ruined his ministry.

In the hands of a power addict, intrigue, prayer, badgering, righteousness, and sanctimonious language can be used to get his way. Suppose you are in a church meeting where an important decision is being discussed. It could be whether to start a building program or call a pastor. You are undecided. Several vocal, intense people express their views. However, their opinions are phrased in the following manner: "After much prayer . . ." "Having searched the Scriptures . . ." "The Lord has told me . . . " and so forth. It is common for those opinions, perhaps no more correct than anyone else's, to carry the day.[3]

True spirituality is a way of being, a way of presenting ideas, that doesn't draw attention to itself. The power addict must draw attention to himself. Pastor Stan fell into this and suffered because of it.

Other addictions and excesses. Addictions tend to occur in clusters. If the basic dysfunctional personality is unchanged, the addict may drop one excessive form of acting out and pick up on another. The other variation is to have several forms of attachments going on at the same time.

Richard is at least 150 pounds overweight. He hoards food, buying his candy and cookies by the carton. Richard hates his work, although his employer seems to value his contributions. He attends church when it is convenient and usually sleeps through the sermon. His wife, Judy, went to the counselor to find out how to cope with Richard's anger and abuse. He is very controlling. Judy has no idea of the family finances, except that they own some real estate. From her husband's continual ranting and raving, it appears there is a huge debt on the properties. Richard evidently is one step in front of the bank's repossessing officer, but he will not tell Judy anything specific.

Richard demands. He is confrontive, belligerent, and arrogant. He never admits he is wrong, and blames others for his mistakes. Richard's father abandoned the family when he was five years old, and his mother took out her frustrations on Richard. Inside this forty-eight-year-old man is a frightened, insecure little boy; but on the outside, he is a roaring lion.

Richard had both a food and power addiction which probably stemmed from the same source, an unfortunate childhood. These addictions are progressing to a destructive and, perhaps, fatal conclusion.

A need to win. The final characteristic of the power addict is the highly competitive need to win. It doesn't matter whether it's a church softball game or Monopoly, the addict has to prevail. Many family members have told me they won't play table games with Dad, Mom, big brother, etc. because a friendly game of Scrabble turns into World War III. If a person's motto is, "Win at any price," I suspect an unhealthy agenda. I have seen fathers who were so competitive they couldn't stand to let their children win footraces or go ahead of the parents in a food line at a picnic.

The power addict is the center of his universe and activities, decisions, and outcomes must revolve around him. He tends to be self-absorbed or selfish and, consequently, unable to encourage others by letting them succeed or have first choice. The belief of the power addict is, "Winning isn't everything, it's the *only* thing."

STAGES OF POWER ADDICTION

Stage One. This is the acquisition phase of the addiction. The person experiences an intoxicating encounter—a business deal is consummated, an award granted, opponent vanquished, or a situation is manipulated to achieve rewarding outcomes. The key element here is an emotional need being met by an experience rather than by people. The euphoric occasion teaches the prospective addict that his feelings can change through a relationship with power. This intense feeling gets mistaken for intimacy and nurturance. The addiction begins when the person falls into a pattern of avoiding pain and intimacy by the use of control and manipulation. The addiction takes hold because he seeks the illusion of relief to avoid unpleasant feelings or situations.

Whether conscious or not, the person associates the activities of power and control with mood changes. He then becomes more preoccupied with using various forms of control to feel better. After a while the uncomfortable feelings become a cue to act out.

In Stage One, the behavior is socially acceptable. This doesn't mean the acting out is healthy. Power used by an addict is destructive. At this point, family, coworkers, or friends may be uncomfortable, but they are not overtly complaining. Also, there are no known violations of the law. People may be emotionally damaged by the actions of the addict, but there are few public outcries.

Stage Two. The addiction is primarily internal in Stage One. At Stage Two the addiction becomes behavioral. The person is more preoccupied with power as a means to feel in control or avoid pain. The behavior is now noticed by others because it is evident the person is out of balance. She is taking risks, offending people, and causing obvious disunity. At this point, labels provide evidence the addiction is progressing. Terms like "cruel," "inconsiderate," "has blatant disregard for others," "watch out she'll turn on you," or "power hungry" would be representative labels.

In this stage, the belief system starts getting acted out in a ritualistic manner. The attachment to power becomes a lifestyle. Time schedules are adhered to religiously. Dress code, room arrangements, and other symbols of power are given high priority. The symbols of power are important, for they define the addict as successful. She amasses clothes, furniture, gadgets, space, titles and, finally, people. By the time the addict begins to see other human beings as symbols, or even as tools who can be useful in the acquiring of more power, the addiction is fully in force.[4]

The addict becomes unusually upset if plans don't turn out as expected because she is so dependent on the anticipated mood change. At this point, the individual is more dependent on her addictive personality than on people or mood changes. Her behavioral commitment to acquiring and maintaining power has become all-encompassing.

Stage Three. The addict now experiences a breakdown in most parts of his life. The addictive personality is totally in charge. Chaos and disarray are the products of continual acting out. In Stage Three, acts of power no longer give the feelings of ecstasy. The addictive personality has recalibrated and become used to the formal rituals and activity. The person is still obsessively preoccupied with power. The rituals and acting out may continue to produce some changes in mood, but the pain never goes away. His behavior is maintained more by habit and fear, than by feelings of euphoria.

The addict now makes dangerous and unwise decisions. People are outwardly concerned about the direction the addict is headed. He has the potential at this stage to engage in life-threatening behavior. His lifestyle is totally devoted to getting high on power and to manipulating those people and things that support the habit.

Howie entered my office with downcast eyes and shuffled his feet as he tried to maintain his composure. It was obvious he didn't have much experience with these kinds of feelings. In a halting voice, he described the events of the past several weeks. Only a couple of days ago he was in the county jail as a result of beating his wife. His memory of the details were hazy, as he tried to portray his frustration and remorse.

A leader in his church and community, Howie was known as a man of conviction. He could always be counted on to head up a project and see it through to the end. Sometimes he would get on people's nerves because of his stubbornness, but it was hard to argue with success.

Unknown to anyone outside his family, his home was like

a concentration camp. Howie kept his wife under total domination, and his kids were always going to the doctor with stomach cramps. What emerged from his story was the picture of a man addicted to control. His vast amounts of fear were hidden behind a fortresslike wall of excessive demands.

What brought the police to his home was a series of altercations with the children that were overheard by the neighbors. Unaware that the police had been called, when Howie heard noises outside his door, he pulled out a revolver and barged outside. The police were ready to shoot when Howie's wife ran out in front of him and begged everybody to put down their guns.

His belligerent attitude, coupled with the reports and evidence of domestic violence, led to Howie's two days in jail. The judge really lit into him during the hearing, and said he must either get help or spend up to two years in jail.

In Stage Three the empire begins to crumble. The addict begins to lose power because of his obsessive need to be in control. There are often problems in the home like those experienced by Howie. Friends, family, and coworkers tend to abandon the addict at this time.

The emotions begin to break down. There are instances of crying, temper tantrums, and fits of rage. The addict becomes highly suspicious, even to the point of paranoia. He thinks everybody is out to get him.

Denial is rampant. Seldom does the power addict voluntarily ask for help. Usually it takes some form of intervention, such as a court order, to get help for the addict.

SELF-EVALUATION
Now it is time to put all of this information about addiction to power to use. Read each of the following questions and answer yes or no to each item. You can do this on yourself or in regard to someone you care about.

TEST FOR POWER ADDICTION

_____ 1. Do you have strong opinions about many things, to the point that people seem put off by your ideas?

_____ 2. Would others say you have difficulty in reaching compromises?

_____ 3. Do you have trouble admitting to your mistakes or faults?

_____ 4. Do your views about issues tend to be rather clear-cut and definite? As far as you are concerned, is there always a right and wrong answer?

_____ 5. Do you struggle to control your temper?

_____ 6. Might other people find your language sometimes abusive? Do you tend to be sarcastic or laugh at the expense of others?

_____ 7. Have you lost your temper or expressed strong anger or outrage more than twice in the past two weeks?

_____ 8. Do you tend to hold your feelings inside without expressing them for long periods, and then let them all out?

_____ 9. Are you aware that when you are angry or resentful you might express those feelings by refusing to cooperate?

_____ 10. Are you a perfectionist? Do other people find you hard to please?

_____ 11. Does it seem that very few people around you seem to know what they are doing and, if given the chance, you are sure you could do a better job?

_____ 12. Do you like being in charge of things?

_____ 13. Does it feel good when you have been successful at arranging a situation so that your expected outcomes are obtained?

_____ 14. Do you seldom say you are sorry or admit you are wrong?

_____ 15. Would you describe your style of getting things done as either "confrontive" or "calculating"?

_____ 16. Do you like to win? Are you highly competitive?

_____ 17. Is it hard for you to accept that somebody else may be better than you?

_____ 18. Have you ever used spiritual sounding terms such as, "The Lord has told me" to help persuade someone to your point of view?

What was your total? If you answered yes to eight or more items, you are probably a Stage Two power addict, and fast approaching Stage Three. Take some steps to change things immediately.

If there were five to seven items that rated a positive response, you are a high risk for being overly attached to power. Don't overlook the opportunity to back off. Continued progression in your current patterns will get you into deep trouble. There are probably already people concerned about you.

Three or four yes answers mean you could get hooked, but may not yet be attached. Be careful. Remember you are a vessel to be used, not the Master Potter.

Creative power. We have seen that addictive power destroys relationships, puts people into bondage, and dehumanizes. It causes disunity. Destructive power makes promises but doesn't deliver, causing frustration and resentment.

So what is the healthy alternative? How can you begin the recovery that would allow God to work through you rather than in spite of you? As with all addictions, recovery from power addiction is not easy. There are no spectacular remedies.

Whether addicted or not, we cannot escape dealing with power. Either we will be a victim of someone else's addiction to power or we will struggle with trying to gain power for ourselves. Even if we have resolved to be a servant rather than a king, the addiction of another person will cause us grief. Sometimes it seems like the work of the kingdom of God never gets done because of the struggle for power.

Biblical power is much different from addictive power. God's version of power restores relationships, sets people free, does not flaunt itself, and produces unity.[5] God gives us gifts for the purpose of edifying and ministering to others. If we find fulfillment in that service, it is to be viewed as a satisfying by-product, not as an end in itself. Unfortunately, the impression of power that comes with service to others has become more important than the furtherance of the kingdom.[6]

God tells us it is foolish to pursue power (Psalm 33:16-19; Isaiah 31:1; Jeremiah 17:5). For example, we are instructed in Psalm 127:1-2, "Unless the Lord builds the house, its builders labor in vain. Unless the Lord watches over the city, the watchmen stand guard in vain. In vain you rise early and stay up late, toiling for food to eat—for He grants sleep to those He loves."

Christians are not called to accumulate power. Rather we are commanded to allow God's power to flow through us. In the flesh we can only approximate this pass-through process. But when we do let go and let God, there is power that creates, redeems, transforms, heals, unifies, strengthens, feeds, serves, resurrects, makes whole, and communicates.[7]

There is a place for creative power or, more appropriately, authority. A father who uses his authority to correct a broken relationship between his children is responding as an instrument of God's power. A counselor who uses her understanding of God's principles to help a couple enrich their marriage is being used by God. The pastor who helps grieving parents deal with the loss of their child is accessing God's power and using his authority correctly.

I would suggest you read Richard Foster's *Money, Sex & Power* for additional illustrations of creative power. Foster identifies the following marks of spiritual power: Love, humility, self-limitation, joy, vulnerability, submission, and freedom. He describes how spiritual power applies to daily life. These are his main points:

- In the individual, power is to be used to promote self-control, not self-indulgence.
- In the home, power is to be used to nurture confidence, not subservience.
- In the marriage, power is to be used to enhance communication, not isolation.
- In the church, power is to be used to inspire faith, not conformity.
- In the school, power is to be used to cultivate growth, not inferiority.
- On the job, power is to be used to facilitate competence, not promote feelings of inadequacy.[8]

We must remember that true power is not ours to keep. We are to accept the authority given to us to be good stewards and then give that power away.

Our model for this process is Christ, and the focus of our efforts is to be a servant. Christ came into this world to serve (Matthew 20:28; Luke 22:27). He instructed us to follow in His footsteps (John 13:4-5). This means we are to take the initiative to utilize our gifts for the service of others. There are bound to be different styles and ways in which this is done. Some servants of God will have more public ministries, others more private. Each one must guard against misappropriating the authority given to him or her.

WHAT TO DO?
Some of the specific guidelines for recovering from your addiction to power will be much the same as for any addiction. The material in the other chapters will supplement what is said here. Remember, all of these ideas contribute to your recovery. You can't take just one or two of these elements and make the program work. It all fits together and

must be used in its entirety.

Admit bondage. The first thing is to acknowledge your bondage. You have become attached to the feelings that power and control can provide. You have reached a point of powerlessness to contend with things the way they are. You must change or you will bring down more destruction.

Ask for help. The next thing to do is tell someone else about your bondage. Avoid delay and denial. It's hard. Pride, especially if you have given all appearances of being successful, will cause you to keep quiet. You've solved other challenges in your life, and are sure you can handle this one. That's a lie. Things are not going well and you need the support and understanding of another human.

It's difficult to find someone, I know. Think about your alternatives: pastor, relative, friend, coworker, business associate, professional counselor, employee assistance program of your company, etc. You are not alone. Others have dealt with this same compulsion. So saddle up your fears and make a decision to share with someone.

It may be advisable to talk to a *professional counselor* who understands addictions. Ask your pastor for a referral, or look in the yellow pages for Christian counseling services. Don't expect a quick solution to your dilemma.

Resolve issues. There are a number of issues that you will probably need to deal with over the next year or two. One is the overwhelming sense of *insecurity* that lies beneath that roaring lion or cunning fox exterior. Your self-esteem has been dependent on productivity. Our culture reinforces that faulty belief. Work toward understanding your identity as a child of God who has been given everything necessary to live an abundant life.

Another important area of reconstruction is your *belief system.* A core belief of most power addicts is, "If I can manage everything around me, it can't hurt me." Another one is, "People will accept me only if I do powerful things. Power is essential to my survival." These are just a couple of many misbeliefs that may be at the core of your thinking. Take some time, probably with the help of others, and examine your belief system for assumptions that have fueled your attraction to power.

You may need to work on resolving *old hurts.* There may have been trauma in your life that has left resentment and bitterness, along with fear and suspicion. These are heavy-duty concerns and need careful attention. Explore them with a counselor. Process your grief. You have a right to be angry about injustice and pain. But at some point you can move on to relinquishing the right to seek revenge or impose punishment. This is called forgiveness, and is necessary to go beyond the hurt. I have written about this as it relates to childhood abuse in *Please Don't Hurt Me.* Other resources are *Healing for Damaged Emotions* by David Seamands, and *Making Peace with Your Past* by H. Norman Wright.

A cluster of issues probably surrounds your difficulty with *anger control.* The goal is learning to be angry in healthy ways. You must learn how to tune in to your feelings. You need to be able to identify all kinds of feelings, not just negative ones. Since most addictive behavior is done to escape pain, work on identifying your sources of pain.

Stress management is an important topic for most power addicts. You have learned to manage stress mostly by controlling someone or something. Take time to learn to relax.

You probably need to learn how to *have fun,* in ways that are not expensive or too demanding. Don't trade one addiction for another. Take time to smell the roses. Learn to be enamored by the small things. See what it's like to put on the eyes of a child and look at a leaf or a rain puddle.

Also, learn to *laugh at yourself.* Don't focus on other people's foibles. Examine your beliefs about your own finiteness. It's okay to have pimples. When you can accept that, you are well into your recovery.

Since control has been your modus operandi for so long, you will have lots of work to do in establishing *communication* with your family and, perhaps, coworkers. Either through counseling or classes, try to develop new ways of relating to your spouse and children. Learn to listen; your family isn't perfect, but they do have some good ideas.

I know it will be hard, but try to *be flexible.* Once old childhood hurts are resolved, it will be much easier. Even though the die is pretty well cast, you can experiment with compromising. Look for opportunities to catch yourself starting to impose opinions on others and try to back off. Take a few risks such as offering partial solutions to problems. Try to blend some of your ideas with those of other people and propose a compromise. It won't always work, but just trying a different approach will be a victory.

Abstinence. Now the really hard part. Give up your power moves. Abstinence is a critical part of recovery. You need to learn how to live from day to day without your fix. This doesn't mean you must become a nonperson, yielding to every challenge that comes along. It does mean, however, that you clearly understand what your power moves are, when you use them, and why you employ them. This understanding will come by taking a fearless moral inventory of yourself and sharing that insight with your counselor and/or support group. Abstinence doesn't happen with awareness alone. You have to put the rubber to the road. You will need to behave differently. People will expect you to operate in the old-fashioned way, so you will have to show them you are in the process of being a new person.

A support group. A support group of some type is crucial to your recovery. You may not find a power addiction Twelve Step group as such, but almost any such group will help. Another option would be to take one of the Twelve Step study guides or workbooks and use it to structure your own group. You could also contact some of the resource organizations in the back of this book for suggestions.

Another idea is a discipleship group of business people, church members, Sunday School class, or a group handpicked by the pastor for an in-depth study of servanthood.

Other addictions. Finally, remember many addictions cluster together. Determine if you have an unhealthy attachment with alcohol, sex, food, work, activities, or anything else. Take the time to specifically work a program for that addiction. Sometimes it seems like an endless battle. There are those willing to stand beside you, and there is a God more powerful than any of them. May you find His serenity.

N O T E S

1. Richard Foster, *Money, Sex & Power* (San Francisco: Harper & Row), 1985, 175.
2. Cheryl Forbes, *The Religion of Power* (Grand Rapids: Zondervan), 1983, 75.
3. *Ibid.*, 76.
4. *Ibid.*, 18.
5. Foster, *Money, Sex & Power*, 196.
6. Forbes, *The Religion of Power*, 94.
7. *Ibid.*, 122.
8. Foster, *Money, Sex & Power*, 201–211.

RELIGIOUS ADDICTION
Is Religion More Important Than God?

● The date was November 18, 1978. The place was Jonestown, Guyana. You may remember the rest. Nine hundred people were murdered or committed suicide at the urging of their leader Jim Jones. Members of the Peoples Temple who had emigrated from California to Guyana had changed from a charismatic church fellowship with good intentions to an autocratic group that somehow became enslaved to their delusioned leader. The result was one of the most tragic events in recent church history, as hundreds of children and adults drank the poisoned concoction.

What made these deeply religious and idealistic people become so captivated that they would be able to drink the cyanide-laced Kool-Aid while seeing dozens of their friends and coworkers literally drop dead beside them? There is probably not a simple answer to that question. From what I understand, addiction to religious practice could explain part of their behavior. They had become so dependent on a leader and his rituals that they could not stop themselves, in spite of harmful or fatal consequences.

In this example, the benchmarks of addiction are present. The process was seductive, insidious, and progressive. It started out appearing to be helpful, but without accountability, it turned into power addiction for the leader and religious addiction for the followers. There were, undoubtedly, moments of euphoria and mystical delight. There were times when God was present, in spite of seriously hampered participants. But somehow, things got out of control and the addiction destroyed everything in its path.

NATURE OF WORSHIP

Let me be very clear here. It is not a sign of addictive behavior to feel the presence of God, to be filled with His holiness, or to experience great emotion during times of worship and praise. There is nothing destructive in the ability to cry, laugh, shout, create music, or to raise the rafters with the joy of the Lord. There are many forms of worship and praise. Each personality tends to select a form of worship that feels comfortable. That should happen. Nothing I am saying is intended to detract from emotion or zeal in church. But what I am gravely concerned about is when our eyes are turned away from God and toward a person or the mechanics of worship.

Jesus was very clear about the object of our worship. "Worship the Lord your God, and serve Him only" (Matthew 4:10; Deuteronomy 6:13). God was insistent that there were to be no other gods before Him (Exodus 20:3). God is a jealous God (Exodus 34:14); He is the one true God (Isaiah 45:21-22; 1 Corinthians 8:4-6). There is no other God to compare with the God of Abraham, Isaac, and Jacob, the One revealed by Jesus Christ (Psalm 89:6; Isaiah 40:18; 1 Timothy 2:5; Hebrews 1:2).

God is to be praised for who He is, and to be thanked for what He has done. Worship is the human response to the divine initiative.[1] We are to exalt God and praise His name (Isaiah 25:1). Worship is our response to the gift of love from the heart of the Father. We are to enter His gates with thanksgiving and His courts with praise (Psalm 100:4).

Because of the crucial nature of worship, Jesus instructed us to "worship in spirit and in truth" (John 4:24). Forms and rituals do not produce worship. God comes and dwells among His people, touching our spirit and freeing us for His glory, praise, and honor. It doesn't matter what form of worship we use as long as we worship in spirit and truth.

DEFINITION OF RELIGIOUS ADDICTION

Addiction to religion occurs when the focus is taken off of God, and emotional priority is given to people or programs. The spiritual addict then uses religious ritual and emotional manipulation as the object or experience to produce a change in mood. The difference is that in true worship, our varied emotional and intellectual response is to the presence of God as facilitated by the forms of worship. In religious addiction, the primary goal is to obtain some type of emotional encounter. One of the only differences between religious addiction and romance addiction is that the latter can be fed by a steaming novel of lust and passion, while the former has a more pious setting and more holy sounding content and motives. Otherwise the dynamics are the same.

The key component in defining an experience or object as addictive is that persistent and continued use brings about negative and destructive consequences. Worshiping God in spirit and truth will result in Christian service (Matthew 5:16), spiritual unity (Romans 15:6), and the bearing of good fruit (John 15:18). True spiritual encounters with God will change us for the better. Resentments will melt (Matthew 5:23-24). The instruction we receive will allow us to mature and reach out to the world in love and wisdom (Colossians 3:16).

The bad fruit of addiction is disunity in families and churches. The name of a pastor or church leader is upheld rather than the Lord. Power and material wealth is amassed for personal use, not for kingdom use. The emotional and spiritual well-being of the addict is harmed rather than healed. There are other destructive elements in religious addiction that will emerge as we look at specific characteristics and functions of being addicted to religious experience.

CHARACTERISTICS OF RELIGIOUS ADDICTION

In this section I will describe various characteristics or symptoms of people who tend to be addicted to religious experience. Not all of the qualities will apply to every person or situation. However, the entire listing can be helpful in determining whether you or someone you love is afflicted.

Highly emotional suggestibility. The person who is vulnerable to religious addiction tends to be very subjective in his experience with the world. He reacts with feelings quickly without always knowing why he reacted the way he did. The person may be more easily moved to tears, joyous laughter, guilt, shame, sadness, and many other emotions. An individual who cries at movies, weddings, baby dedications, and Eagle Scout award ceremonies is also vulnerable to being manipulated by religious ritual.

Again, may I say there is value in having strong feelings and emotional reactions to a beautifully sung choir anthem, or experiencing tears when a speaker portrays a soul-wrenching illustration. We are meant to have and display feelings. However, I believe there is a line of demarcation after which some people become more concerned with getting an emotional "hit" than they are in growing in spirit and truth. It is for these people I am concerned.

The religious addict needs an authority figure to tell him what to do and how to think. Even a well-educated, sophisticated person can have this quality when it comes to spiritual issues. It's as if there is a small child inside who needs structure, rules, and expectations clearly established by an authority. And once that authority figure has established him or herself, the addict is remarkably vulnerable to further suggestions or influence. Usually there is a power-addicted religious leader and a suggestible follower who match up, just as a drug dealer and user would connect. They need each other, and feed each other's addictions.

Blind belief. Along with suggestibility, religious addicts tend to be easily persuaded. Sometimes this is because of intellectual naiveté; but bright people can also be gullible and overly trusting. Addicts do not think things through completely; they don't discern truth effectively. The writer of Hebrews tells us, "But solid food is for the mature, who by constant use have trained themselves to distinguish good from evil" (Hebrews 5:14).

The mature Christian, one who is not vulnerable to addiction, will seek out teaching and associations that hold God up as the only Source of spiritual knowledge. Teachers and pastors are vessels God uses to communicate truth, but we must always remember the Master Source. The addictive personality is looking for easy solutions or ways of behaving that help cover up pain and weakness. This makes him want to believe teachings that propose health, wealth, and prosperity, but without the accompanying dedication to a life of commitment and sacrificial service.

Black-and-white thinking. The religious addict tends to place ideas, values, preferences, and people into clear-cut categories. People are either good or evil, honest or unlawful. There is not much in between.

Alice loved her church and her pastor. She sang in the choir, taught a Sunday School class, and attended most of the women's activities. Alice struggled with a difficult marriage and children who had trouble in school, and she tend-ed to be overweight. Her emotions were like a roller coaster. One day she was happy to the point of euphoria. The next day she might be exceedingly depressed.

Her friends began to notice some disturbing changes in Alice. She talked constantly about the religious TV and radio programs she monitored daily. Then she started engaging her friends in discussions about specific and detailed points of doctrine. Alice would increasingly refer to one particular radio teacher in the defense of her position. If a friend brought up a contradiction or raised a question about the concept Alice was presenting, she would get angry and insulting. Alice would often call into question the spiritual commitment of her friends when they refused to agree with her position. In fact, she told one woman who had been a friend for eight years, and a Bible study leader, that she doubted if the friend was actually a Christian. All of this rigidity took place over a bit of unimportant religious dogma, and is very typical of a religious addict's style.

Theological isolation. Alice's story, unfortunately, did not end there. After repeated run-ins with most of her friends over her newfound doctrinal beliefs, she stopped coming to church. Instead, she stayed home and concentrated on listening to her radio teacher. She signed up for a correspondence course written by this same instructor. She stopped tithing to her local church and sent the money to the radio evangelist instead. After a while, Alice had cut off all contact with people in her local church and concentrated exclusively on her radio personality.

The key here is an unhealthy intolerance for the views of others, combined with theological and social isolation. The addict wants no part of anything that doesn't give the emotional fix. Just like the other forms of addiction, religious addiction becomes preoccupied with the exclusive rituals and customs associated with the leader. The addict becomes very protective of that leader, and will do anything to ensure his continued availability.

Obsessive participation. The addict has found a mood change brought about or heightened by participating in various religious activities, and so these activities receive even more attention. Things like fasting, prayer, attendance at meetings or services, public testimonies, or confessionals are given almost exclusive priority. Families are ignored while Mom goes to meetings night after night. A diabetic continually fasts contrary to medical advice. A story of emotional trauma is repeated time after time in public meetings. Prayer becomes an obsession to the exclusion of family, work, or the responsibilities of ministry.

Each of these activities is intended to be a significant and necessary part of the Christian's spiritual life, so how can they be suspect? Jesus gave instruction on both prayer and fasting (Matthew 6:5-18), pointing out the importance of motive. To the extent that either is being used to our own ends, it is done with unhealthy motivation. Both prayer and fasting can be used to try to manipulate God, or to make people think we are more pious than we are.

Confession, testimony, prayer, fasting, or public worship are to center on God. They must be a response to God, and not to our need to blot out pain or to experience a short-lived feeling of euphoria. You can pretty well know if any of these activities have crossed over into the obsessional when you find yourself thinking about the activity rather than the end product. If it draws you closer to God, restores your soul, refreshes your spirit, enhances growth and maturity, the fruit tells you it is good.

Harsh and angry attitudes. Intolerant, dichotomous thinking usually progresses to an angry, critical response toward others who do not share the same collection of beliefs and behaviors. This can include an acerbic attitude toward "nonbelievers"—those outside any church, as well as other sects or denominations.

The addict is very judgmental of others. She has come to believe that she is being nurtured by the activities of the religious environment to which she has become attached. It is these activities or beliefs that take on the power to create the mood change. This gives the focus of the addiction a great deal of power. It is now essential for the addict to cope with life—pray, believe, or participate—in a particular way. It is part of the ritual. Whatever is seen as a threat to that mood-altering experience is the enemy. Be it a lifelong friend or spouse, the enemy must be corrected or eliminated. The leader must be protected. This is why so much anger and hostility are directed at the opposition.

This harsh perspective often spills over into criticism of institutions such as schools, community agencies, and government. The addict can be very opinionated, usually following the prompting of her spiritual authority. The reaction is that all teachers are bad, all politicians are evil, and all persons of a different ethnic heritage are prejudiced.

Strong attempts to persuade. The addict won't stop talking about his beliefs or opinions. He compulsively talks about God and religion from his narrow point of view. He will quote Bible verses to support his opinion, and often make reference to his leader.

He will also try to persuade others to his point of view. The addict will cover the same ground with the same person again and again, alienating the other individual. He doesn't know when to stop. He just knows what experiences have brought him emotional ecstasy, and he wants others to try them also.

Symptoms of tension. Religious addicts have not found the permanent peace and inner fulfillment they were anxiously seeking. As a result they suffer many physical symptoms of poor stress management. Chronic headaches, back pain, high blood pressure, overweight, underweight, anxiety attacks, depression, sleep disorders, and allergies are all possible indicators.

God doesn't promise us freedom from pain or disease. But there is evidence that contented Christians have fewer health problems, including most of the above symptoms.[2] Faith works when it is placed in God, the Great Physician.

FUNCTION OF RELIGIOUS ADDICTION

Attachment to form, rather than to the substance of religious participation, serves a number of functions for the addict. The following discussion will give you an idea of how religious acting out can help reinforce the addictive personality.

Avoidance of intimacy. We have seen how other forms of addiction serve to escape intimacy. This is also true for religious addiction. By becoming involved with the activities of faith and practice, a person can avoid experiencing a real encounter with the mind and spirit of another believer or with God Himself. A preoccupation with ceremony or doctrine can keep God at arm's length. It might be similar to a teacher who becomes so immersed in his subject that he fails to realize he is not communicating with his students.

Religious habits can also put the addict to sleep, thus allowing him to avoid being convicted by God for change and service.

Elimination or avoidance of pain. Most of us tend to avoid going to the dentist or doctor. We don't like the procedures necessary to diagnose and treat illness. We respond the same way to the Great Physician. We fear what will happen in a close communion with God: old submerged feelings may rise to the surface causing pain and confusion; unresolved issues with family may come back into our awareness, reminding us of the anguish of yesterday.

Awareness and treatment of the source of pain is sometimes difficult. But the addict also makes it more intimidating by her faulty beliefs: "I am such a terrible and unworthy person that God would not accept me the way I am. I must do these things to earn His acceptance. Then I can share my pain, and He will do something about it." These misbeliefs, and others like them, keep the addict in a state of private terror. "I cannot reveal my innermost being to God. In the meantime, I will focus on spiritual activities, and maybe they will keep the pain away." The emotional energy is then directed to participating in the forms of sanctimonious and devout observances. Pain is suppressed, the avoidance behavior is rewarded, and the addictive cycle is perpetuated.

Elevation of moods. Who hasn't gotten goose bumps during the singing of the "Hallelujah Chorus," or been moved to tears during the moving portrayal of the Easter story? For the religious addict, feeling good is not the by-product of church involvement but the goal. In this sense, it is just like skydiving or compulsive running. The experience produces a change in mood that excites and invigorates. The endorphins in the body are activated and an enhanced state of arousal is achieved.[3]

It probably is an oversimplification to explain mood change exclusively in biochemical terms, but the change is very real. The thrill of seeing hundreds of people move forward in response to an altar call has a strong chemical similarity to ingesting morphine. Does this invalidate the experience? Not at all. It simply illustrates the complex creation of God which follows laws and principles of biochemistry that we only barely understand. We would probably agree on the need to moderate the amount of food, exercise, or sex in our lives. We also need to moderate the amount of sensory stimulation, including that which happens in church. It can be addictive and, unless we continually focus our attention on the Creator, can get us into trouble.

Compliance to authority. To a surprising degree, when an authority figure says "Jump!" many of us will obediently ask, "How high?" Some time ago, a severe flood hit an area of Illinois, requiring the mobilization of the National Guard and various emergency services. At the height of the crisis, a young man arrived on the scene, announced he was from an obscure state agency, and proceeded to take control of the emergency. City work crews, the fire department, local police, municipal officials, and the National Guard followed his orders with dispatch for several days, evacuating entire neighborhoods. Finally someone thought to check and found out the man had walked in off the street. He had no experience or training in emergency services, just a history of unemployment and psychological problems.[4]

The local officials were red-faced, but most people would have responded the same way in that kind of situation. Most people have a willingness to obey someone who seems to be in authority.

Christians have even more of an inclination in this direction because we are instructed to submit to the authority of the church (1 Corinthians 16:16; Hebrews 13:17). Only a few people escaped the Jonestown massacre; and some who did try to escape were shot.

There are two important principles here. First, leaders are responsible to take initiative to utilize their gifts for the service and benefit of others. They are not to lord it over those entrusted to them (1 Peter 5:3).

Second, followers must exercise enlightened understanding in their response to authority. We are to be self-controlled and alert (1 Peter 5:8), as well as discerning of powers and regulations that are hostile to the way of Christ (1 Corinthians 12:8-10; 1 John 4:1; Colossians 2:6-23). This is not an easy task. Leaders can be persuasive and deceptive. An enlightened submission would have us live in subordination to human authority until it becomes destructive.[5] God has promised us the ability to discern evil spirits, but the believer must be watchful, and draw on the entire body of gifts to remain protected.

Group pressure. If you keep a well-manicured lawn or wear the latest fashions, are you conforming? It depends. If you maintain your lawn only to avoid complaints from your neighbors, you're yielding to social pressure. If you wear the clothes you do because you genuinely like the style, that's not conformity. If your choice is dictated by the fact your friends would question your taste, then you're conforming.

The same is true in religious participation. If the addict engages in certain rituals or espouses various beliefs because of group opinion, it is conformity. If one has thought through the options and made a conscious choice, the resulting behavior is not as likely to be addictive.

The power of group pressure is significant. Psychological studies have found that compliance results from subtle, implied pressure. Compliance is affected by explicit rules, requests, and commands. If, for example, the informal rule in a congregation is that women should never wear slacks in church, the women will probably comply, even if they have certain reservations about the validity of the expectation.

Addictive personalities tend to have less resistance to group pressure because they are so heavily dependent on the approval that compliance to group expectations brings. Religious addicts want to feel good. Participation in the particular activities of the fellowship brings approval. The approval comes directly in comments and compliments and indirectly by seeing other people engage in the same behaviors. Addicts receive tacit or implied sanction for conforming.

Evidence of spirituality. Religious addiction provides evidence that the person is truly "spiritual." Based on the assumption that one's spirituality can be judged by outward conduct, the myth is perpetuated by the addict's belief system. "To be a true believer, one must: pray, fast, witness, attend, believe, say, etc. I do those things. Therefore, I am a true believer." The logic usually continues with, "The more I do these things, the more spiritual I will become."

Compliance and participation in the religious activities give the person an identity. He is seen as one who believes and is faithful in his practice. This behavior serves to validate to himself and others the reality of his spiritual commitment.

STAGES OF RELIGIOUS ADDICTION

As with the other forms of addiction, there are three stages the religious addict goes through—acquisition, loss of control, and breakdown of his life.

Stage One—Acquisition. This stage begins with an intoxicating religious experience. It could be a healing service, a conversion experience, or a close personal encounter with another person in a spiritual context. For the addict, this euphoric experience gives the *illusion* of being present with God. He receives comfort, nurturance, and joy from the experience. And the *experience*, not God, takes on a heightened interest.

Addiction begins when the individual begins to focus on anything other than God. He then begins to seek out certain experiences to avoid unpleasant feelings, to find identity, or conform to group expectations.

This is the beginning of the mental preoccupation with the object or experience that leads to a change in mood. The key that separates true spirituality from addiction is the addict's progressive allegiance to a person, institution, ideology, or experience, rather than to God.

Stage Two—Loss of Control. During this stage the addict is progressively less able to control when she starts or stops a behavioral pattern. There is a compulsive quality to her efforts. The frequency of acting out increases as the body develops a tolerance to former levels of activity, and needs more of the emotional experience to get a high.

The addict becomes more ritualistic in her participation, going to meetings, praying, fasting, giving money, etc. when her circumstance suggests otherwise. There can be an almost daze-like quality to her demeanor. She can't explain to you how or why God has asked her to do something; she just knows she is supposed to do it.

The difference between legitimate and addictive giving, for instance, is that the legitimate is prompted by God and not by manipulative pleadings. Also, nonaddictive giving has the blessing of God. That's why we can't necessarily judge at the outset whether a person is being responsible or not; we don't know the inner leading of the Lord. But we can wait and see if the seemingly unwise stewardship of time or resources turns out to be contradicted by God's providential provisions.

During Stage Two, family and friends know something is wrong. Large amounts of time are unaccounted for, and explanations do not match up to reality. The addict is much more dependent on experience than rational thought.

Another thing that can happen is a spiritual deadening. In

spite of all the addict's spiritual participation, he seems shallow and without substance. His claim to spiritual growth doesn't match up with fruit in his life. He doesn't seem content; rather, he is restless, constantly searching for a better way to serve God or his spiritual leader.

During Stage Two, there is often a gradual granting of power to a specific leader—a local pastor or media evangelist. This often begins by donating money and is usually progressive. In extreme cases, such as was true for the members of People's Temple, the addict may turn over all assets to the leader or the organization. Accompanying this financial commitment, the addict will become increasingly focused on the belief, doctrine, and personality of the leader, giving him or her godlike qualities and power.

Stage Three—Life Breakdown. Now the addict is totally preoccupied with his cause. His mood-altering activities no longer produce euphoria, but he continues out of fear of withdrawal.

At this point, life outside of the cultlike organization has lost most of its meaning. Personal and family life is likely in chaos. If the addict's immediate family does not share his addiction, the family may break up. For the addict the responsibility to the cause or experience is greater than commitment to marriage.

Many parts of the addict's life are upset. She may be having problems at work, and may even lose her job because of the involvements. This is where irrational acts, such as drowning a child, attempting suicide, or committing a crime, may occur out of the distorted belief that she is being led by God.

In part because of the disapproval by friends and family, she becomes extremely suspicious. People may, in fact, have tried to stop her from misappropriating resources, or have discouraged her attendance at more meetings. She becomes more secretive, often lying about her whereabouts, knowing the truth would bring more conflict.

Violation of previously held values takes place at Stage Three. The addict may commit adultery, incest, fail to report a crime, cover up actions of the leader, lie, or resist outside accountability.

All of this progression leads to the total destruction of everything the addict formerly believed and held dear. Life is now in complete chaos. The addiction is in total control, and outside intervention is probably necessary to get the addict out of the clutches of the obsession.

SELF-EVALUATION

Here is an evaluation tool to help you decide if you, or someone you are concerned about, has an addiction to religious experience. Read each item and respond with a yes or no.

TEST FOR RELIGIOUS ADDICTION

_____ 1. Do you tend to be emotional and sometimes react to events without understanding why?

_____ 2. Do you have consistently strong and intense emotional responses to events and situations in religious settings, i.e., weddings, funerals, musical productions, worship services?

_____ 3. Have you found that you can be easily led by a strong personality?

_____ 4. Can you become so convinced about the truth of something that you have a hard time listening to other ideas or opinions?

_____ 5 Do you tend to hold opinions and values that are fairly clear and definite?

_____ 6. When you become convinced of the truth or value of something, do you tend to want to talk about it frequently?

_____ 7. Have you stopped attending a church in the last three to six months because you got the feeling people weren't accepting your ideas about spiritual issues?

_____ 8. Do you find you are rather intolerant of people outside of your present fellowship or support system?

_____ 9. Do you feel guilty if you don't attend most of the services of your fellowship? Or, if you follow a radio or TV teacher/preacher, do you feel guilty if you are unable to listen to most of the programs?

_____ 10. Have you increased the amount of money or resources you have given to your church or spiritual leader, against the advice of family or friends?

_____ 11. In spite of frequent participation in spiritual activities such as prayer, fasting, worship, etc., do you still experience a lack of fulfillment and purpose?

_____ 12. Are you suspicious of family, friends, or coworkers who do not share your current religious beliefs or activities?

_____ 13. Do you spend lots of time trying to convince others of your ideas or the ideas of your teacher?

_____ 14. Are you experiencing physical complaints such as headaches, back pain, upset stomach, fainting spells, sleeping or eating problems, anxiety, or depression?

_____ 15. Have your friends and family questioned your current spiritual involvement?

_____ 16. Have you experienced major disruptions in your life such as separation, divorce, legal action, or major church divisions, as a result of your spiritual beliefs and participation?

If you answered yes to eight or more items, you could very well be in Stage Three of addiction. Immediate intervention and change is necessary.

Three to seven yes answers reflect a strong possibility of religious addiction. It is strongly urged that you consider acknowledging your need and take steps to get help.

One or two positive responses do not mean anything significant. Look at the specific items and carefully evaluate whether there is anything for which you should be concerned.

WHAT TO DO
Acknowledge the problem. For religious addicts, the starting point is the same as for all other forms of addiction — admitting your dependency on a mood-altering experience. Spiritual experience has become _the_ source of nurturing, and religious ritual the focus of your life. Everything else has been sacrificed or compromised for the sake of spiritual highs. This powerlessness has made your life chaotic and unmanageable, and your compulsion has separated you from God. When you are in bondage to something of the world, even if it has the appearance of religiosity, you cannot love and serve God (Matthew 6:24). You have two masters and cannot serve both.

Addiction is seductive and progressive. You may not have realized how unmanageable your life has become. If you are compulsive, your thinking is distorted; you may be unaware of how destructive and troublesome your behavior is. Your habit patterns may have developed in such a gradual way that you didn't see it happening. Your good intentions and holy aspirations have led to a dependence on a particular personality and/or to an attachment to religious activity apart from true communion or worship.

Addiction to religious experience can serve several purposes. It can help you avoid intimacy with God as well as with fellow humans. Your addiction can facilitate the avoidance of pain and give you an emotional arousal. It can help you comply with the expectations of leadership and of others in your fellowship. Finally, compulsive religious activity can seem like evidence of spirituality. When your behavior serves these functions, it is unhealthy and counterproductive to the real intentions of God for your life.

Talk to someone who can help. After acknowledging your addiction and your inability to control it, you need to tell somebody. Identify a mature friend, counselor, or pastor who will listen to your story. Do not select the pastor or leader of your fellowship, if he has been a part of your acting out pattern. If a leader has taken advantage of your trust and helped perpetuate your following, he generally will not be receptive to your desire to change. Select someone you know to be strong in the Lord, experienced in addictive issues, and supportive of your intentions.

It may help to write out your story. Begin with your earliest recollections of how the progression began. Read back over chapter 1, as well as this chapter, to get some ideas about what to include. This needs to be an honest look at what your addictive behaviors have done to you and others. It is not intended as confession of all your mistakes. You might try responding to these questions:

- When and how did you first start to use religious activity to fix yourself from avoiding intimacy, escaping pain, or accessing good feelings?
- Can you describe any increased usage of religious acting out during times of increased stress? Give some examples.
- Somewhere along the way, you probably knew your behavior was out of control, and was interfering with other parts of your life. When and how did that happen?
- What did you ever do to try to change your behavior? How did other people react to your attempts?
- Can you describe any increased frequency of your behavior as a result of your system building up a tolerance and needing more sensations to provide even minimal satisfaction?
- Read through the material on the three stages a religious addict tends to progress through and describe how you fit the progression.

Now go share your responses with the person you have chosen. It will be hard, but it needs to be done. The first goal is to share your awareness. Then allow yourself to receive some support from him, and proceed to do some planning about what to do next.

Find a support group. In addition to a counselor/sponsor type of individual, you need to join a recovery group; perhaps a Twelve Step group such as Al-Anon or Overcomers Outreach would be great. Even a group such as Religious Anonymous might be appropriate. Check any group carefully, to make sure it keeps God as a central focus, and is not intent on stamping out any form of faith. The group will provide some support, as well as instruction, for the difficult road to recovery. Read chapter 9 which describes the Twelve Steps and you will see how they can help.

Stop the behavior. Abstinence is a key requirement of recovery. If you have been attending numerous meetings, watching daily programs, or spending a specific number of hours in certain activities, my suggestion is to stop everything you have been doing. It's like going cold turkey, I know. Instead of participating in your addiction, spend a balance of time in four areas: (1) Reading of Scripture and related material, (2) meditation, (3) conversation with your counselor or sponsor, and (4) attendance at the support group.

• The first area is to spend time in God's Word with the purpose of letting His truths speak to you. Scripture is a lamp·to your feet (Psalm 119:105). It is food to help you grow (1 Peter 2:7). God's Word is a life-giving force (Ezekiel 37:7). It gives hope (Romans 15:4), and it will help probe and illuminate your specific needs (Hebrews 4:12). I don't believe you can spend time in the Bible with the specific intent of having God speak to you and have that time prove fruitless.

I would recommend that you read Richard Foster's *Celebration of Discipline.* He covers the inward disciplines of meditation, prayer, fasting, and study in a way that focuses on God Almighty and His Son Jesus Christ. It is an excellent presentation by a man of integrity, and will give you specific direction for turning your attention away from the activities and ritual of religious compulsion.

• Foster also gives specific helps on how to approach meditation. Look at what he has to say and try using it. An example would be to take a passage of Scripture and reflect upon it. Let's take just a portion of Colossians 2:6-23 for illustration:

> *Since you died with Christ to the basic principles of this world, why, as though you still belonged to it, do you submit to its rules: "Do not handle! Do not taste! Do not touch!" These are all destined to perish with use, because they are based on human commands and teachings. Such regulations indeed have an appearance of wisdom, and with their self-imposed worship, their false humility and their harsh treatment of the body, but they lack any value in restraining sensual indulgence.*

Contemplate what that means to you and your situation. Ask God to open this passage up to you. How does it apply to your beliefs? What are the implications for your walk of faith and your history of compulsion to rules, rituals, doctrine, authority figures, and activities? Now go on and read Colossians 3:1-17. This gives the positive side of what you are supposed to be and do. It is in dramatic contrast to a life of rules and compulsive compliance.

• The third recommendation is to spend time with a counselor. There are many issues to cover. Earlier pain or trauma, resentments, low self-esteem, faulty belief systems, and many other topics which contributed to your lack of control will need attention.

• Finally, these insights can be integrated and supported by a group meeting. The interaction there will help you deal with relapses, reclaim lost hope, gain encouragement, and provide many other good and necessary benefits.

N O T E S

1. Richard Foster, *Celebration of Discipline* (San Francisco: Harper & Row), 1978, 138.
2. Vincent Bozzi, "A Healthy Dose of Religion," *Psychology Today*, November 1988, 14–15.
3. Janet Hopson, "A Pleasurable Chemistry," *Psychology Today*, July/August 1988, 29–33.
4. Wayne Weiten, *Psychology Themes and Variations* (Pacific Grove, California: Brooks/Cole), 1989, 616.
5. Foster, *Celebration of Discipline*, 108.

CHAPTER EIGHT

ACTIVITY ADDICTION
Do You Need an Adrenaline High?

● Two figures stand precariously near the edge of the roof of a 700-foot bank building. It is an unusually bright, sunny, crystal clear day. Robin and Brian fastidiously check their parachutes, making sure everything is correctly rigged. As they look at the tiny automobiles slowly moving about on the snow-clogged streets below, they are eager to jump.

After some nervous laughter and banter, Robin says, "We're in the groove. Let's go for it."

Then the young men step out on the end of some scaffolding overhanging the edge of the building. Brian counts down "Ten . . . three, two, one," and they step off the edge. Time seems to stand still as they experience a sense of weightlessness and paradoxical feelings of fragility and power in the same instant. Exhilarated by the experience of total control, their lives seem at once supreme and valueless.

When the chute opens, Robin is pleased. He gracefully navigates his floating assemblage through a half circle, deliberately drifting to a clearing in the mall below. Both men land near several passersby. Wide-eyed with curiosity, one onlooker blurts out, "What planet did you come from?" Robin's nonchalant reply was, "Oh, you liked it, huh?"

Brian joins his friend, and the two hop in the getaway car. The police arrive four minutes after the daring fait accompli.

In the aftermath, Brian and Robin feel intoxicated by the wine of success. The pristine ecstasy of free-fall is replaced by group celebration, euphoria, and bliss.[1]

Francie, age thirty-six, is an executive assistant to a government official. Six mornings a week, she rises before 7:00

and heads for the health club where she spends the first hour of her day in a vigorous aerobics class. Then she goes to work. At noon, she leaves her desk, changes her clothes, and goes next door to a small gym, where she pedals furiously for forty minutes on a stationary bicycle. Three nights a week, she joins her husband for a Nautilus and bicycle workout at the health club.

On the rare occasion when she has an early morning meeting, or when she has a lunch appointment, Francie gets annoyed. She even was impatient with her husband because he wanted to go away for a weekend; that meant she would have to miss her Saturday morning aerobics and muscle-toning exercise class.

Francie resents any disruption of her exercise routine. "It makes me angry," she says. She admits she's hooked. "I'm addicted. When I'm exercising, I'm at my best. I have stamina. I'm happy and able to accomplish more. When I couldn't exercise due to an injury, I was upset and depressed."

Every day millions of us engage in activities just because they give us pleasure. We seem drawn to work, money, shopping, exercising, playing sports, and many other things because we feel stimulated whenever we do them. A positive mood change takes place while engaging in these experiences. For many this leads to a compulsive attraction to these events. Those same exercise freaks will also experience discomfort or withdrawal pains when they are deprived of the chosen activity.

In the previous examples we saw two types of experiences that can bring about feelings of euphoria or excitement. Shopping, giving blood, and jogging can produce similar sensations. Many perfectly legitimate and beneficial activities can be addictive, if carried too far.

I will organize the discussion into two categories. The first is risk-taking and engaging in thrilling and adventurous activities. The second is compulsive or excessive activities such as exercise, running, shopping, and even donating blood.

THRILL-SEEKING
When we become excited, either through anger or fear, our brains signal hormone-producing glands to release chemicals that prepare us for fight or flight. The adrenal glands produce cortisol, a chemical that increases blood sugar and speeds up the body's metabolism. Other messages to the

adrenal glands result in the release of the amphetamine-like stimulant epinephrine (adrenaline), which helps supply glucose to the muscles and brain, and norepinephrine, which speeds up the heart rate and elevates blood pressure.[2]

The psychological by-products of this chain reaction are noticeable increases in one's feelings of physical prowess and personal competence and strong sensations of pleasure. In many ways, the state of biological and psychological readiness produced by stress is mimicked by the effects of stimulant drugs. Drinking two or three cups of coffee will double the level of epinephrine in the blood, for example. The same reactions can happen by riding a roller coaster or watching a great theatrical performance.

What is so attractive about risk-taking and fear-inducing situations? In terms of brain chemistry, the sky diver seeks the same mind-altering escape from depression, stress, or fear of failure as any other type of addict we have discussed. Whether jumping from the top of a 700-foot building, driving a speedboat at 100 miles an hour, or using cocaine, self-induced changes in neurotransmission may lead to a path of compulsion, loss of control, and continuation in spite of harmful consequences. Some experts believe stress-drunkenness causes more overall harm to society than alcohol.

I have talked to teenagers who go to the most savage horror movies in town because they "love to be scared." These confessions support the idea that risk-taking and fear-inducing situations can be very attractive.

Researchers have found that the increased level of neurotransmitters in the synaptic junction of the brain can be accomplished by a sky diver jumping out of an airplane or by a cocaine user ingesting drugs.[3][4] While the biochemical process is slightly different, the end effect is the same. The mood of the person is elevated. We have seen that any activity which is repeated for the specific purpose of altering a person's mood has the potential for abuse.

Just as with substance abuse, the body develops a tolerance to the thrill seeker's attempts to keep the body in a constant state of emergency. During the maintenance phase of addiction, the person begins to feel "normal" only while actively pursuing arousal activities. In skydiving or in watching horror movies, the techniques that produced an incredible high in the early stages no longer provide the same intensity of feeling. In order to achieve a sustained elevated state of arousal, a sky diver must attempt more daring and dangerous maneuvers. At this point, he is faced with a choice. Either he must find new ways to enhance the chemical changes or give up the addictive process and attempt a life of abstinence. Giving up the arousal activity puts him into withdrawal. Then the thrill-seeker feels depressed, apathetic, and is very vulnerable to a relapse.

Not everyone who engages in arousing activities loses control. But because there is both a physiological and psychological potential for addiction, caution in all things is advised. The admonition given by Paul, "Each of you should learn to control his own body in a way that is holy and honorable," is very appropriate for our cultural setting where there are so many mood-altering experiences from which to choose. The fact that brain chemistry may be responsible for affecting our moods doesn't remove our responsibility. We must realize the important part our thoughts and choice play in determining how far the sequence goes. We don't control the brain chemistry once it starts, but we can choose to monitor our habits and lifestyle so as not to let mood-enhancing activities get the upper hand.

CHARACTERISTICS OF THRILL-SEEKERS

A thrilling adventure such as white-water rafting, hang gliding, or mountain climbing will elicit squeals of delight from some and shrieks of horror from others. Not everyone is drawn to this type of mood-altering experience. Some people thrive on excitement while others become disoriented and upset by it. Of people observed during natural catastrophes such as fires and floods, about fifteen percent of the people are able to function in an organized, effective manner; about seventy percent display varying degrees of disorganization, but manage to function somewhat effectively. The remaining fifteen percent, however, are so disoriented by the situation that their coping is completely ineffective. They may wander about aimlessly, scream, or collapse.[5]

Researchers have found that there is a thrill-seeking personality called Type T. Such persons opt for excitement and stimulation whenever they can find it, either through intense physical or mental activity.[6]

Type T people tend to be creative, risk-taking extroverts who prefer more sexual variety than average. They like experimental or impressionistic art. They may have had legal problems as teenagers, possibly are seen as hyper-actives, and are more likely to be reckless drivers. Intel-lectually, Type Ts are creative thinkers who have a talent for seeing ideas and solutions from a unique perspective. They can approach a problem from many angles and have many entry points into its solution. They can shift from abstract to concrete forms of thinking, and they tend to translate images into words more easily than other peo-ple.[7]

The thrill-seeker will be unhappy and ineffective in a highly structured work environment that emphasizes routin-ized performance and rigid lines of authority.

High sensation types will tend to behave more fearlessly when confronted with fearful situations such as heights, snakes, or darkness. They take more risks with their money. Of course, the thrill-seeking personality will be more likely to engage in dangerous sports such as motorcycle riding or scuba diving. One interesting finding is that when both the husband and wife are thrill-seekers, they are inclined to have a very satisfying marriage. I guess that means the theme for a married team of parachutists would be, "The couple that dives together, thrives together."[8]

Thrill-seekers can channel their propensity toward risk to the benefit of society in such ways as becoming astronauts or test pilots. We might presume Sir Francis Crick, Nobel Prize-winning codiscoverer of DNA's structure, and Evel Knievel, daredevil entertainer, would be mental and physi-cal Type T personalities. I can't help but wonder if the Apostle Peter was a Type T.

On the other hand, certain conditions could lead a Type T predisposition to engage in pointless self-destruction or bi-zarre criminal behavior that destroys others. Rasputin, the Russian political manipulator, infamous bank robbers Bonnie and Clyde, or mass murderer Ted Bundy, might be examples of the destructive Type T.

SELF-EVALUATION
These questions, adapted from a Sensation Seeking Scale de-veloped by Dr. Marvin Zuckkerman, may help determine if you fall into the thrill- or sensation-seeking category of in-terest. Answer yes or no to each of the items. This test will not tell if you are addicted, just whether you tend to have a low or high need for sensation.

TEST FOR THRILL-SEEKING PREFERENCES

____ 1. Do you have very little patience with dull or boring people?

____ 2. Do you prefer art that shocks or jolts the senses over one which provides a feeling of peace and security?

____ 3. Would you like to ride a motorcycle?

____ 4. Would you rather have lived in the unsettled days of history?

____ 5. Do you sometimes like to do things that are a little frightening?

____ 6. Would you like to be a part of new and different approaches to life?

____ 7. Is one of your major goals to live life to the fullest and to experience as much as possible?

____ 8. Would you like to try something like parachute jumping, hang gliding, or scuba diving?

____ 9. Do you tend to dive or jump right into the ocean, lake, or cold pool?

____ 10. On a vacation, do you like to camp out rather than stay in a motel?

____ 11. Do you prefer people who are emotionally expressive, even if they are a bit unstable?

____ 12. Would you prefer a job that requires travel more than one which requires you to work in one place?

____ 13. Are you invigorated by a brisk, cold day?

____ 14. Do you get bored seeing the same faces every day?'

If you answered yes to one to five items, you have a low need for sensation. Scores of six to nine are average, and ten or above are high. Low scores suggest your life is pretty routine. You may like a little stimulation, but on the whole, you don't seek out variety or change. Average scores indicate you may need sensation in one or two areas of your life, but your desires are not high enough to cause any problems. High scores indicate you need a great deal of variety and change, as well as a high intensity of experience. You will need to monitor yourself carefully to make sure your needs for new and intense experiences do not lead to trouble.

COMPULSIVE ACTIVITY

Thrill-seekers compose one type of activity addiction. I have chosen to describe a second category which includes behaviors that are not quite as spectacular, but which can become every bit as addictive. The physiological workings may be the same for getting high from running or spending money, as for jumping out of an airplane. Yet, I guarantee more readers have exercised or spent money than have experienced a 5,000-foot free-fall. Thus, I think we need to take a look at experiences common to the majority, which can result in our being addicted to our own adrenaline.

The process starts when the body produces large amounts of adrenaline and related hormones under stressful fight or flight conditions. This adrenaline creates a surge of energy to help us respond to the stressful challenge. This surge of energy feels good. Pain is suppressed and we feel excited and powerful.

Following the law of effect, we tend to repeat activities that are pleasurable. If that cycle is repeated too often, however, it is possible for us to become hooked on the "adrenaline high" to the point we crave it. This prolonged search for arousal can lead to physiological and psychological distress. Research shows that hyperarousal of the adrenaline system is a major factor in coronary and artery disease. Headaches, gastric problems, ulcers, and high blood pressure are also symptoms of stress damage. If we do not learn to minimize our dependence on the adrenaline high, the pleasure we derive from even healthy endeavors can be a slow form of self-destruction.[10]

Many Christians would be astonished to find they were addicted to their own hormones. How would it sound in the next prayer meeting if it were announced that Deacon Johnson was requesting prayer for an addiction problem? I can hear it now—the pastor comes to the pulpit with a grim expression on his face and makes the following shocking announcement: "Due to circumstances beyond his control, Deacon Johnson has become consumed by the evil habit of fishing. He would not listen to the pleadings and warnings of his family, so last Friday the elders of the church met with Mr. Johnson in his home and completed an intervention procedure. He was shocked and angry in the beginning, but after being confronted with the reality of his addiction, Mr. Johnson agreed to enter treatment. The first thing Monday morning, he was admitted to the Northwest Angler's Treatment Center where he will be dried out and detoxified. He apologizes to the congregation for all the trouble he has caused, is embarrassed by his loss of control, and asks for your support during his difficult road to recovery."

Okay, maybe I'm exaggerating a little bit here. But we are vulnerable to developing addictions without even being aware of it. Here are some examples of several forms of activity addiction.

ADDICTION TO EXERCISE

No one denies the benefits of exercise. People who exercise look and feel better. They gain energy and can be more productive and creative. Their resistance to disease is enhanced; exercise is the best way to control weight. It is also necessary to healthy functioning. For example, stress on the long bones of the legs prevents loss of bone minerals. The circulatory system must be stressed by lengthy exercise in order to promote adaptations that increase the heart's efficiency. But exercise can be abused, and can even be hazardous to your health.

If you like to exercise and are not sacrificing anything in the process, you're probably not in jeopardy. The problem comes when you begin to abandon other things. If you let your job or relationships take second place to exercise, if you place yourself in physical danger, or if you get depressed and miserable when you can't exercise, then you are in trouble.

There is a progression evident in sports or exercise participation. Often the decision to take up a sport is based on a *dissatisfaction* with a sedentary lifestyle. For example, the person looks in the mirror one day and decides to do something about the spare tire around his middle.

The second stage is one of *initial success*. The person achieves some self-satisfaction from participating in the activity. The reluctant novice goes out with a group and shoots a ten-point buck and suddenly becomes a confirmed hunter. The fly fisherman experiences the excitement of seeing the rainbow trout rise to the surface and strike the fly, and then he feels the jolt on the line. The battle lasts only five minutes, but by the time the six-pound fish is in the creel, the adrenaline rush has had its effect, and the fisherman is hooked for life.

In the case of running and jogging, success can be attained very soon because these sports do not require complicated athletic skills. The initial success can be privately measured by the individual running a mile without stopping or jogging for half an hour. Because of the physical exertion the new athlete is able to sleep better, enjoy eating more, or finds depression lifted.

The third step toward excess involves a heavier *investment* in the sport with time and money. Athletic equipment or sporting paraphernalia is purchased. The latest in aerobic fashion wear is acquired. More classes are taken until several nights a week are devoted to practice or participation. After a while it begins to affect one's family and social life.

The fourth step in the progression involves the *reinforcements* that the person receives for achievements related to the sporting or exercise endeavor. For example, a friend comments on the weight loss; the increased energy level shows up in work productivity; an improved sense of well-being comes over the participant. Entrance into a new subculture is another reinforcement. Taking up a sport is a social event; many people will work out with a companion, and go to social or recreational outings together. Perhaps the team meets for pizza after the game. Even if one is a solitary runner, that fact can become an item for conversation and social interaction.

It has also been shown that running can produce morphine-like substances called beta-endorphins that deaden pain and enhance one's sense of well-being and self-esteem, resulting in the so-called runner's high.

Like any form of addiction, exercise can be used to escape other tensions in the person's life. One runner said, "I did my best running while I was going through my divorce."

In a leisured society that lacks many new frontiers to explore, some people turn to risky sports such as hang gliding, skydiving, or mountain climbing in a quest for new and exciting experiences. Extreme tests of endurance in running, swimming, or other sports may serve a similar function.

If involvement continues at the level of step four, the activity will remain a rewarding and satisfying experience. However, if the fifth step is taken the participant may become unbalanced and truly addicted. At this point a *confusion* occurs between means and ends. The sport becomes a goal rather than a means to physical and emotional well-being. The person begins to lose sight of why she initiated the activity in the first place.

In the sixth step, sport or exercise participation becomes *excessive*, and the confusion between means and end is

complete. Other activities, such as work and family responsibilities, are subordinated. The addict is now willing to sacrifice other parts of his life, and the addiction is in charge.

If the progression continues, the person moves to the
seventh step. This is where major *illness or injuries* result
from excessive participation. Cardiovascular problems, mus-
cular-skeletal injuries such as shin splints, sprained ankles,
runner's knee, chronic back pain, and other manifestations
become chronic or acute. Hormonal problems can include
amenorrhea and adrenal deficiency. Disturbed kidney function and gastrointestinal distress are among other physical
difficulties that can result from excessive exercise.

Withdrawal symptoms also begin to appear because the
addict cannot maintain the activity level. Because the body
has to adjust to a reduced level of adrenaline or endorphin
output, lethargy, depression, and pain enter the picture. The
compulsion to resume the activity is extreme, but the body
may not be able to cooperate because of the injury. The
addict is now caught in a dilemma.

The illness or injury, along with withdrawal symptoms,
leads the addict to assess his behavior. In step eight, some
soul-searching begins. The addict may seek advice from a
friend, physician, or counselor. At this point the contrast
between the sedentary, preaddictive lifestyle, and one in
which exercise is all-consuming, is very apparent.

Step nine involves making a *choice.* After the review, the
addict will either compulsively try to continue former levels
and types of exercise, substitute a new activity that does not
make the same physical demands, but still gives satisfaction,
give up all activity, or opt for some type of moderation. This
step may involve a lot of vacillation. The addict may quit, lay
off a while, but then resume with a vengeance. He may try
moderate participation, but fluctuate between compulsive
and appropriate levels of activity.[11]

Exercise is a two-edged sword. It can cure or injure you.
It is a prescription item that has to be taken in the proper
doses. In small doses, it can be curative. If taken too heavily,
it can addict you and harm you.

SELF-EVALUATION
Take the following quiz to find out if your sport or exercise
activity has become an obsession. Answer the following
questions yes or no as truthfully as you can.

TEST FOR EXERCISE OR SPORT ADDICTION

_____ 1. Do you exercise every day, regardless of weather, illness, schedule, or injury?

_____ 2. Do you get so used to your exercise routine that even very important events are intrusions? You start fitting your life around your activity instead of fitting your activity into your life.

_____ 3. Are you depressed if you miss a scheduled workout, and become irritable and cranky?

_____ 4. Do you not feel right, good, or complete if you haven't exercised?

_____ 5. Is your sport or activity the main topic of your conversations?

_____ 6. Do you have a strong preoccupation with keeping track of your times, repetitions, weight, wins, or other measures of success?

_____ 7. Do you spend a lot of time arranging your diet to match your exercise needs?

_____ 8. Do you spend a great deal of time thinking about your physical health?

_____ 9. Is it possible your activity is a way of escaping from personal or family problems?

_____ 10. Do you get depressed over minor injuries?

_____ 11. Is your commitment to exercise causing personal problems, such as arguments with your spouse, or complaints from your children or friends that you're never around?

_____ 12. If you miss a workout, do you try to make it up late at night, or by doubling up the next time?

_____ 13. While working, do you fantasize about your sport or activity?

_____ 14. Have you been criticized for spending too much time or money on your activity?

_____ 15. Is your work suffering because meetings with colleagues or clients would conflict with your exercise schedule?

_____ 16. Are the only friends you now spend time with those who share your activity?

If you answered yes to more than one or two items, you need to adjust your commitment to the activity. It is possible a perfectly good thing has possessed you and is robbing you of your freedom to choose.

WHAT TO DO

Excessive exercise can be as harmful as no physical activity at all. Here are a few brief suggestions for curbing this addictive form of acting out.

Recognition. You must acknowledge that participation in the sport or activity has become excessive in terms of time, money, or necessity. There is no good reason, other than compulsion, for you to continue your present level of participation. Take some time right now and write out a statement acknowledging your state of affairs. Go ahead. It won't kill you, and it will get you started on your recovery.

Admission. Next you must admit that there have been personal and social costs attached to your level of participation. You have punished your body, distanced yourself from friends and family, and ignored other priorities. Continue your writing by listing all of the disadvantages or problems caused by your participation. Then list all the advantages. There are some, but too much of a good thing is dangerous.

Understanding. Both your intellectual and emotional self has to recognize the possible biological, psychological, social, and professional consequences of continued excess. The previous step appealed to your cognitive side. Now we need to communicate with your addictive personality. What are the fears, insecurities, beliefs, expectations, and purposes that were part of the motivation for exercising? Try to let the little person inside of you do the talking here. Spend some time in prayer and meditation. We know about the physiological part of activity addiction. That is a reality. But what is your inner child getting out of all of this?

Resolution. You now need to come to a decision about your participation in the activity. It may be wise to talk this over with your physician. What can you legitimately expect your body to handle at this point in your life? Get some reliable recommendations. Don't try to be your own expert here. Your opinions are biased and come from an addictive point of view. If there are emotional issues, make contact with a therapist and work them through. Do some reading on the subject. Two books are mentioned at the end of this chapter. See if they would help.

Try abstinence for a while, even if your body has not given off red flag warnings. Don't go to your class or activity for a few days. Do something else that's not as demanding. The day following your missed activity, notice you haven't gained twenty pounds. Your body is not atrophied into a prune. Keep paying attention to the results. It is not a matter of life and death for you to miss or moderate your activity.

Also spend some time thinking and writing down all of the aspects of your being that are not a part of your exercise or activity. Think about personality traits, values, emotional, social, spiritual, and intellectual features that exist totally apart from your physical being.

Don't leave the spiritual dimension out of your consideration. God wants you to have self-control and He will help you with the difficult task of regaining proper balance.

Moderation. Once you have worked through the above steps, you're ready to decide whether to continue your activity in moderation, stop it altogether, or substitute another activity.[12]

SPENDING ADDICTION

There was a knock at the door that Sally had been dreading for five years. "I've come to talk to you about the forged checks," the investigator said. "I am with the district attorney's office."

Sally then confessed to embezzling $5,000 from the company where she used to work. After being booked into the county jail and later released, Sally was forced to admit she was a compulsive spender.

There are probably millions of men and women of all ages, races, and socioeconomic groups who have a compulsive attraction to spending money—even money they don't have. The key difference between compulsive spending and harmless or recreational shopping is that addictive spending is out of control. You don't control when you start or stop the activity. Shopping can achieve the status of a mood-altering addiction characterized by powerful mood swings from intense arousal to blissful satiation. However, it is also often followed by depression and remorse. Recreational shopping does not have the same degree of mood swing, or the post-episode depression.

Like all other addictions, there are both physical and emotional contributions to the progressive urge to "shop till you drop." The adrenaline rush over finding the bargain of the year, or discovering a unique or long sought after item, can become something we want to repeat.

The urge to spend can also be linked to feelings of low self-esteem. We may try to clothe ourselves in purchases to make up for that missing ingredient. We tell ourselves, "Maybe I will really be happy if I have this possession." This is an illusion fed by our materialistic society and advertising campaigns, but we literally "buy" into it.

These false beliefs were part of what led Sally to spend money she did not have on items she did not need. "My self-image never allowed me to say, 'I can't afford it.' " In college she had to have the "perfect" clothes in order to fulfill her image of the perfect person. The same thinking followed her into marriage as she bought all the things she thought a "perfect young couple" ought to have.

Often the initial high experience connected with the newly acquired symbols of self-love fades into "buyer's remorse." Shopping euphoria turns to depression and feelings of unworthiness. After the binge, addicts confess that they didn't discriminate between purchases. They find they bought clothes that didn't fit or weren't appropriate for their needs. Often binge purchases are not used. They may sometimes be returned to the store, only to have the addict take the refunded money and go off on another spree. Other addicts, afraid that storekeepers will recognize them as binge-purge shoppers, keep the items and cling to them much as a young child does a security blanket.[13]

Shopping is probably used a couple of million times a day as a method for coping with depression or other negative feelings. For example, one young opera singer would spend $200 on a pair of shoes whenever she performed poorly at an audition. It finally dawned on her it would be much cheaper to make arrangements to meet with a supportive friend instead of heading to the mall.

Unlike excessive drinking or drug use, society condones and encourages excessive spending. This makes it even harder for the chronic spender to face up to her problem. Sometimes it takes hitting the bottom, like Sally did, for the addict to realize she has a problem.

SELF-EVALUATION
Here is another set of questions to identify if shopping or spending money is a compulsive activity for you. Answer each item with a yes or no.

TEST FOR SPENDING ADDICTION

_____ 1. Is shopping or spending money one of your primary forms of having a good time?

_____ 2. Do you tend to buy things on the spur of the moment?

_____ 3. Have you bought items such as clothes, tools, knickknacks, craft materials, art projects, decorations, home improvement supplies, etc. that sit in a closet or storage room for weeks or months before you ever use them?

_____ 4. Do you spend more than thirty percent of your take-home pay to cover your loans and credit cards?

_____ 5. Do you sometimes use one line of credit to pay off another?

_____ 6. Have you sometimes hidden your purchases or lied about them so your family wouldn't know you had been shopping?

_____ 7. Will you tend to buy something that is on sale, because it is such a good buy, even though you have very little use for it?

_____ 8. Have you lied about how much something cost, or when you bought it, so your friends or family would better accept your reasons for buying it?

_____ 9. Have you felt guilty, remorseful, or anxious after a shopping spree?

_____ 10. Have you often taken back things which you purchased on a buying binge?

_____ 11. Have you intentionally gone shopping to lift your spirits or help deal with depression, rather than because you really needed something?

_____ 12. Do you have trouble making your paycheck last from one pay period to the next because of your spending patterns?

If you answered yes to three or more of these items, consider the fact you may have a compulsive attraction to spending money.

WHAT TO DO
If you have a tendency to spend money for the wrong reasons, there are several things you can do to regain control.

Admit your problem. Admit you have difficulty with shopping and tell somebody about your situation. Don't leave out any details. Give them the whole story. They can't be your ally if they don't know the truth.

Organize your finances. Make arrangements to get together with a person who can help you organize your finances. This will include making a budget, and figuring out an accountability system so you can follow it.

Cut up your charge cards. If you have been writing insufficient-fund checks, close your checking account too. Pay for purchases with cash and pay bills with money orders or certified checks.

Stop the behavior before it starts. Remember the opera singer who met with a friend instead of buying shoes? Find out when you are vulnerable to wanting to go shopping. Look for cues that trigger your spending sprees and take evasive action. Divert the energy when you are tempted to shop. Go to the movies, talk with a friend, take a walk. But don't go to the mall.

Improve your self-concept. Do some things to make you feel better about yourself. Identify all of your addictions and make a plan to eliminate them. Go to school, do volunteer work, upgrade your work skills, enrich your marriage, improve your ability to communicate, or deepen your spiritual understanding and relationship with God.

Get some help. You may need to talk with a professional counselor and/or join a support group for addictive behaviors. Several organizations such as Spender Menders and Debtors Anonymous are listed in the reference section. Contact them for information and referral assistance.[14]

GENERAL COMMENTS

I am sure Jesus knew about our susceptibility to addiction. He said, "Come to Me, all you who are weary and burdened, and I will give you rest. Take My yoke upon you and learn from Me, for I am gentle and humble in heart, and you will find rest for your souls. For My yoke is easy and My burden is light" (Matthew 11:28-30).

Activity addiction is a situation where our focus is taken off of the important priorities of living. Instead of looking to Christ for our comfort, we turn to excessive exercise or spending money to make us content. As we have seen, that effort can progress into serious problems.

Jesus modeled calmness and peace, which is the opposite of addiction to an adrenaline rush. A furious squall hit the Sea of Galilee and threatened to swamp the boat Jesus and His disciples were using to get from one side of the lake to the other. Sleeping at the time, Jesus was awakened and asked if He cared that they all might drown. He immediately quieted the storm and then asked, "Why are you so afraid? Do you still have no faith?" (Matthew 4:40)

We often feel just like the terrified disciples: "God, don't You care that my life is out of control? Can't You see the storm that is raging in my life? Help! Do something before I drown!" God does care, but we need to give Him the opportunity to take control rather than try to do it ourselves.

There are no easy solutions to escape the clutches of addiction. It's not just a matter of trusting God and finding all of the storms are quelled. Turning to God for help is the first step, however. Behind the tyranny of the urgent is an assumption that the world will collapse if we don't keep pace. Until we give up that faulty thinking and heed Christ's words, "Do you have no faith?" we will remain enslaved.

Our addictive personality says, "It is never enough."
Christ answers, "I am enough."

N O T E S

1. Harvey Milkman and Stanley Sunderwirth, *Craving for Ecstasy. The Consciousness & Chemistry of Escape* (Lexington, Mississippi: D.C. Heath), 1987, 94.
2. *Ibid.*, 97.
3. *Ibid.*, 98.
4. Sidney Cohen, *The Chemical Brain. The Neurochemistry of Addictive Disorders* (Irvine, California: Care Institute), 1988.
5. Milkman and Sunderwirth, *Craving for Ecstasy*, 110–111.
6. Frank Farley, "The Big T in Personality," *Psychology Today*, May 1986, 44–52.
7. *Ibid.*, 48.
8. Milkman and Sunderwirth, *Craving for Ecstasy*, 116.
9. Gail Kessler, "How Much Sensation Do You Need?" *Glamour*, April 1986, 182–185.
10. Archibald Hart, *Adrenaline & Stress* (Waco, Texas: Word Books), 1988, 86–87.
11. Hartley Hartung and Emile Farge, "Compulsive or Excess Sports," in *Behavior in Excess*, S. Joseph Mule, ed. (New York: The Free Press), 1981, 297–308.
12. *Ibid.*, 307.
13. Milkman and Sunderwirth, *Craving for Ecstasy*, 108.
14. Patrick Pacheco, "When You Can't Stop Shopping," *McCall's*, December 1986, 174–175.

CHAPTER NINE

STEPS TO RECOVERY
How Can You Overcome Your Addiction?

● "Jesus looked at them and said, 'With man this is impossible, but not with God; all things are possible with God' " (Mark 10:27).

Regardless of your addiction, the road to recovery is through Jesus Christ. All of the insight and understanding in the world will fall short of what is necessary, unless that knowledge is placed in the hand of the Son of God. Then He can guide your path along the way to sobriety and serenity.

This book is written for Christians and those who value Christian traditions. The emphasis of this discussion will be on the biblical basis of the principles found in the Twelve Steps. Some might say, "If you are really a committed Christian, you wouldn't have an addiction problem." I wish that were true. The reality is that there are thousands of addicted Christians. They believe that God exists and Jesus is their Saviour. But they are still under bondage, not because the promise of God's grace is not true, but because they haven't learned how to appropriate that grace into their daily lives. I believe the truth inherent in the Twelve Steps can be a powerful tool for learning how to apply the truths of God's Word to the life of the Christian who is struggling with addiction.

The Twelve Steps are really restatements of biblical principles. Their genius is that they are simple enough for a drunk to understand, but profound enough to keep all of us spending a lifetime learning how to apply them. Let's look at each step and see how the content can be used by God to help us find freedom from addiction. The wording of the steps has been taken from *The Twelve Steps for Christians*, by Friends in Recovery. Other valuable help appears in workbook form in *The Twelve Steps—A Spiritual Journey*, by Friends in Recovery, and *God, Help Me Stop*, by Claire W. I would suggest you get at least one of these books and use it by yourself or with a group. Instructions for organizing and running a support group are included with the Friends in Recovery books.

At the end of each Step, I will ask a few questions to try to help facilitate your interaction with the material. I would suggest you get a notebook to record your responses. This journal can be very beneficial as you gain new insights and identify old suppressed feelings.

In chapter 1 we saw that addiction is a cyclic route that goes from pain to pleasure to pain. Recovery begins when the acting out is no longer sufficient to numb the pain. An addict will not consider changing his ways if the object or experience is still producing a mood change or helping him cope with stressors. William Lenters has said it this way, " 'What works, works,' is the addict's motto. 'As long as the booze numbs the pain, pour me another one. As long as the adulterous liaison makes me feel good, let's keep meeting in cheap hotels. As long as religion eases the guilt, practice it ever more obsessively.' An addict does not see the light of day without experiencing the bleakness of night."[1]

The ability to recover from addiction and the freedom to make responsible choices are linked to pain. We will not grow, convert, or repent, unless something stops us dead in our tracks. Look at the biblical precedents. Moses had to be confronted by the presence of God in a burning bush. David repented for his adultery with Bathsheba only after being confronted by Nathan. Jonah had to spend three days in the belly of a whale before he got his directions straight. Paul had to be blinded by God on the road to Damascus before he would give up persecuting Christians. The Philippian jailer had to experience a violent earthquake and the threat of punishment for letting his prisoners escape before he came to be saved.

In this sense, the addict's intense pain can be seen as an instrument of truth that removes the veil of denial. This idea is wonderfully illustrated by C.S. Lewis in his portrayal of Eustace Clarence Scrubb in *The Voyage of the Dawn Treader*. Eustace was a real egghead and despised by most everybody. He was self-centered and had a knack for saying just the right thing to antagonize people. Then he joined Lucy and Edmund in an adventure that took them aboard an unusual sailing ship named the *Dawn Treader* to a remote mountainous island. One evening Eustace left the campsite and eventually wandered into the lair of a recently deceased dragon. Since he was lost, Eustace spent the night sleeping on a pile of treasures that had been hoarded by the dragon. Before he went to sleep, Eustace placed a bracelet around his arm, but awoke the next morning to the rather disturbing fact that he had actually become a fire-breathing dragon. It seems that sleeping on a dragon's hoard with greedy, dragonish thoughts in his heart, had turned Eustace into a dragon.

Eustace eventually found his way back to his friends. (It was made much easier now that he could fly.) There were some communication problems, but finally Eustace was able to convince everybody he was really their friend. It seemed Eustace's character had been rather improved by becoming a dragon, and he tried very hard to be helpful. Yet, he really didn't want to remain a dragon and the bracelet around his arm proved quite painful.

Then one night Eustace had an encounter with Aslan, the lion. Aslan offered to ease the pain of the injured leg by bathing it in a bubbling well. But first Eustace needed to have his ugly scales removed. He tried himself and managed to remove several layers of the rough and wrinkled skin. Then Aslan said, "You will have to let me undress you." Eustace was afraid of the lion's claws but was nearly desperate now. The first tear was so deep, Eustace thought it had gone right into his heart. But Aslan succeeded where Eustace could not, and the scales were removed to reveal the little boy beneath. Aslan then threw him into the water. It smarted like everything for a moment and then became perfectly delicious.

Then the lion dressed Eustace in new clothes and undragoned him. "It would be nice and fairly nearly true, to say that 'from that time forth Eustace was a different boy.' To be strictly accurate, he began to be a different boy. He had relapses. There were still many days when he could be tiresome. But most of those I shall not notice. The cure had begun."[2]

This delightful metaphor depicting the healing touch of

the Lion of the tribe of Judah leads us from the function of pain to an examination of the first step.

STEP ONE

Admit that we are powerless over the effects of our separation from God — that our lives have become unmanageable (Romans 7:18).

This step requires acknowledgment of helplessness and recognition that we need help. There are two parts to our admission. First, we admit that we have developed an addiction, or a skin of scales, contrary to the desire of God. Second, we admit that our lives are, and will continue to be, unmanageable if we try to take the ugly scales off by ourselves.

Our compulsion is a form of idolatry. When we are in bondage to things of this world, we are not free to love God. Our attachment to a mood-altering object or experience separates us from God. This compulsion has a damaging influence in every area of our lives. It threatens and confuses our entire being. When we deviate from the plan God has for us, our despair, chaos, and disorder can cause emotional and physical disorder (Psalm 6:6-7).

It is hard to give up control and admit to personal powerlessness. The acting out gives us a feeling of control. For a long time it has been very predictable and effective in bringing us escape from pain and feelings of euphoria. But as the addiction progressed we became less able to control when we started or stopped the acting out.

Step One gives us the chance to regain control by renouncing our attempt to control. It sounds like a paradox, but that is the way it works. When we acknowledge that what we *thought* we knew was not really what we *needed* to know (1 Corinthians 8:2), we begin to remove the veil of denial.

When Bartimaeus approached Jesus for healing, it was obvious he was blind. Yet he had to openly ask Christ to heal his blindness (Mark 10:51). Step One asks us to make the same acknowledgment.

• Take some time now and write out your response to "I admit I am. . . ." Then say it out loud. Better yet, take this step with someone you trust and tell them who and what you are.

- Look up these verses: 2 Corinthians 12:1-10; Ephesians 3:16; Hebrews 11:32-34. What do they say about strength in weakness? How does this apply to you?

STEP TWO

Believe that a power greater than ourselves can restore us to sanity (Philippians 2:13).

The purpose of this step is twofold. The first is to demonstrate that God is a power greater than we. The second is that God wants to be a vital part of our daily lives. Many addicts have given a general assent to the existence of God and accept the possibility that He is out there somewhere. But now the goal is to realize that He is a personal God who cares about everything that happens to us. And because He cares, He will restore us to sanity and away from our addictions.

The opposing forces in this step are doubt and hope. Doubt, which has ruled the belief system of the addict, has two allies—fear and anger. As children we may have been taught that God is a type of heavenly critical parent who should be feared. God was someone who punished us if we were wrong. That fear only served to fuel the shame and guilt which arose from the cycle of addiction. So we acted out again to escape the feelings of fear and guilt, only to have those same feelings intensified when the ecstasy subsided. We have to get beyond the idea that God could never love someone who behaved in such a "wrong" manner. We have nothing to fear when we put our trust in Him. "So do not fear, for I am with you; do not be dismayed, for I am your God. I will strengthen and help you; I will uphold you with My righteous hand" (Isaiah 41:10).

The second ally of doubt is anger. We may harbor anger at God because He let us down, as a child who prayed for safety and was still abused by a family member. Many addicts have rejected God because He did not give relief from their pain. I cannot deny the pain and I cannot explain why such things happen. I just know God can work and be glorified even in the middle of our problems. He understands our anger. This is a journey to recovery, not an overnight trip. The process of identifying our fear and anger will take a while, but as the journey proceeds we will find doubt turning to hope.

The process of turning doubt to hope comes, in part,

because of where we place our faith. That's why a portion the size of a mustard seed is sufficient. For years, we have placed our faith in our own ability to do things right. That was the wrong place to put the belief.

The issue of doubt or faith is not a matter of degree or amount, but where you place it. By placing it in God, you are assured of help and healing (Matthew 14:22-34).

God can accept us in the process of learning to believe. Remember when Jesus healed the boy with an evil spirit? The boy's father brought the child to Jesus and asked if He could do anything for his son. Jesus replied, "Everything is possible for him who believes." Immediately the boy's father exclaimed, "I do believe; help me overcome my unbelief!" Then Jesus proceeded to cast out the evil spirit and the boy was made whole (Mark 9:23-24). We can start the journey even if we have doubts. God will accept us wherever we are.

Step Two gives us new hope as we begin to see that help is available if we simply reach out and accept the gift our Lord has to offer. All that is required of us is a willingness to believe. What follows as we proceed through the steps is a process that will bring His power into our lives and enable us to grow in love, health, and grace.[3]

- Read these verses relative to God's power to heal: Psalm 34:18-22; 40:1-2; Matthew 19:26; Luke 4:18-19; Ephesians 3:20. What do they say to you? What are your feelings and reactions as you read these verses?
- Describe your doubts about God. What are your fears? Do you have feelings of anger toward God? Write down these responses in your notebook or journal.
- If you are ready, complete this statement: "I have come to believe. . . ."

STEP THREE
Make a decision to turn our will and our lives over to the care of God as we understand Him (Romans 12:1).

In Step Three we entrust our lives to God. This is a natural progression from Step One where we admitted we were powerless, separated from God, and that our lives had become unmanageable. In Step Two we affirmed God was the only power that could restore us to sanity and sobriety.

Now we prepare to turn over the steering of the ship to God. We commit to doing His will. We plan to follow His direction rather than our own. This is the "let go and let God" Step. Our goal is to be able to turn over to God responsibility for the big things in our life, as well as the smaller details, and to do so with complete abandon.

If this makes your head spin, and the progression is going too fast, slow down and take your time. You need to be ready to turn your life over to the care of God. However, this won't do any good if you feel pressured or go through the actions as a matter of ritual.

This decision can be made a little easier when we admit we haven't done such a wonderful job so far. But the same drive for self-knowledge and control that compelled Adam and Eve to eat the forbidden fruit propels us to take back the controls. Our self-will has kept God at a distance up to now and the idea of surrender is frightening. If, for example, we have experienced violence or trauma in our past, we are going to be extremely reluctant to risk trusting anyone, including God. This isn't going to be easy. It is a process that comes gradually, as we slowly learn to turn our very being over to Him and trust the results.

"Trust in the Lord with all your heart and lean not on your own understanding; in all your ways acknowledge Him and He will make your paths straight" (Proverbs 3:5-6). This verse captures the essence of Step Three. Our own understanding has only led to compulsive acting out. Now it is time to make an affirmative decision. We must move through the veil of denial which shuts out the light of God. Our path will be illuminated and made straight by choosing to let God be our guide.

Trust happens with experience and over time. At this point you may only be able to give God responsibility for the most painful parts of your life. That's okay. Give Him what you can. As He proves faithful in some things, you will be able to hand over more parts of your life.

Abraham is listed in the Hebrews 11 roll call of the heroes of faith. That faith did not develop overnight. Abraham was one of the Bible's greatest worriers. He worried that foreign kings would covet his beautiful wife and kill him to get her (Genesis 12:12-13; 20:11). He worried about shortages of grazing land for his animals (Genesis 13:6-8), about retaliation (Genesis 15:1), about a lack of an heir (Genesis 15:2-3), about God's possible inability to honor His covenant (Genesis 16:1-4), and about God's intent to destroy Sodom and Gomorrah (Genesis 18:23-33).

In spite of God's promises, Abraham worried that he and Sarah were too old to bear children. After the birth of Isaac, Abraham worried that God wouldn't know which of his two sons to use in fulfilling the promise of many descendants (Genesis 21:11).

It took time and experience for Abraham to become a man of faith. He grew from his experiences just like we can. There were times Abraham took matters into his own hands, just like we do, with disastrous results. But God was patient, Abraham became obedient and he learned to trust God. We can experience the same steps to belief.

Part of our being tells us we will become nothing if we turn our lives over to the care of God. The truth is that the more we are able to depend on God the more independent we become. Our reliance on God is actually a means of gaining the true emotional and spiritual independence we all seek.

- Write down your reactions to the idea of turning over your life to the care of God. How does the prospect of doing that make you feel? How about your fear and doubt?
- Now read these verses: Psalms 34:8; 118:8-9; Proverbs 16:3; Jeremiah 29:11-14; Matthew 11:28-30; John 10:1-10; 14:12-13; Galatians 2:20; Revelation 3:20.
- In light of your addictive history, describe how the ideas in these verses apply to you.
- Write out a response to God, "I have made a decision to. . . ."
- Share that decision with someone. It will be difficult, but God will reward your effort.

STEP FOUR
Make a searching and fearless moral inventory of ourselves (Lamentations 3:40).

In this Step we examine our behavior and expand our understanding of ourselves. This journey of self-awareness begins with Step Four and continues through Step Seven. During this time we will prepare a personal inventory, discuss it with others who share our journey, and ask God to work in spite of our failures.

We now begin to look at the dark side of our character, to identify and understand our character defects and see how these have controlled our behavior. Denial is our biggest enemy, but up till now it has been our closest companion. Denial has given us many defenses and maneuvers to protect ourselves from the reality of our addictions. An honest inventory of our self-defeating patterns gives us a tool for learning a great deal about our compulsion and its consequences.

An inventory is not a history. It is an itemizing of stock currently on hand. Viewing the inventory this way makes it easier to prepare a fearless description because we have no need to be afraid of the consequences of understanding our potential. Yes, the wages of sin is death (Romans 6:23), and we all have sinned (Romans 3:23; 1 John 1:8), but the gift of God is eternal life and freedom from bondage and the consequences of our choices (John 8:32; Romans 6:23).

Our inventory may reveal characteristics we don't like to acknowledge, but awareness allows us to hand them to God and to receive deliverance. An inventory includes both strengths and weaknesses; we need to accept ourselves rather than judge. The information we gain is another step in the journey to recovery. We are the beneficiaries of honesty. The more truthful and complete we are about the inventory, the more we will gain from the process.

How can we go about this step? Putting our thoughts on paper is valuable and necessary. Writing focuses our thinking, and allows us to zero in on the important understandings. Writing helps get in touch with feelings and beliefs that were outside of our immediate awareness.

- Write down your resentments, fears, guilt, shame and a detailed account of your compulsive acting out. List specific examples of your behavior including *who* was involved in the situation, *when* the incident took place, *where* the behavior took place, and *what* you did.
- Review your desires, thoughts, motives, and actions in terms of the Seven Deadly Sins—pride, greed, lust, anger, gluttony, envy, and laziness. Look at these with the common denominator of fear. Pride can be the fear of humility, greed the fear of not having enough, and lust the fear of intimacy. Anger can be the fear of powerlessness, glut-

tony the fear of pain, envy the fear of having no identity, and laziness the fear of failure. How do these possibilities relate to your history?

- You might want to consider doing a concise, simple form now and a more detailed version later in the program when you have more understanding. Don't try to do it all at once. If your circuits overload, put it down and come back to it later.
- If you don't seem to be getting anywhere on your own, even after praying for God's help and direction, you may want to contact a pastor or counselor for help. The assistance of an outside party can help greatly.
- Here are some verses related to this step: Lamentations 3:40; Psalm 139:23-24; Matthew 7:1-5; 2 Corinthians 13:5-6; 2 Peter 1:5-10; James 1:19-21; 1 John 4:18. Refer to them and others as you do your inventory.

STEP FIVE
Admit to God, to ourselves, and to another human being the exact nature of our wrongs (James 5:16).

Now that we have identified the character traits that led to our compulsive behavior, we can relieve the burden of guilt and shame. This is done by admitting to ourselves and another person our faults, and confessing our wrongdoings to God. We aren't just telling God what happened, since He already knows. Instead, we are acknowledging these things are wrong and repenting of them and making a decision to turn away from our sin.

Confession is a requirement. Without confession we cannot receive God's forgiveness and be freed of the judgment of guilt (Acts 3:19; 1 John 1:9). We don't admit our wrongdoing to God for His benefit. It is an opportunity to gain access to God's mercy and grace. He is patiently waiting for us to confess how we have been trying to run our own lives, and failing miserably.

By confessing our faults to God, several results occur. Our prayers will be answered (2 Chronicles 7:14), our sins are pardoned (Isaiah 55:7), we are given life (Ezekiel 18:21), we are comforted (Matthew 5:4), and we are given the gift of the ministry of the Holy Spirit (Acts 2:38).

Probably the hardest part of Step Five is admitting our wrongs to another human being. This can be real scary. Allowing another person to see our hidden parts is very uncomfortable. We have spent years behind a mask of pretending to be somebody we were not. Now we are being asked to take off the mask and be real. In the words of the Velveteen Rabbit:

> "What is REAL? Does it mean having things that buzz inside you and a stick-out handle?"
>
> "Real isn't how you are made," said the Skin Horse. "It's a thing that happens to you. When a child loves you for a long, long time, not just to play with, but REALLY loves you, then you become real."
>
> "Does it hurt?" asked the Rabbit.
>
> "Sometimes," said the Skin Horse, for he was always truthful. "When you are Real you don't mind being hurt."
>
> "Does it happen all at once, like being wound up," he asked, "or bit by bit?"
>
> "It doesn't happen all at once," said the Skin Horse. "You become. It takes a long time. That's why it doesn't often happen to people who break easily, or have sharp edges, or who have to be carefully kept. Generally, by the time you are Real, most of your hair has been loved off, and your eyes drop out and you get loose in the joints and very shabby. But these things don't matter at all, because once you are Real you can't be ugly, except to people who don't understand."[4]

This delightful story illustrates the process of becoming real. It doesn't happen all at once, and it doesn't happen if we remain hidden from sight. Step Five asks us to take the risk of having most of our hair loved off by the receptive listening of a dependable person. We are instructed to confess not only to God but to one another. Step Five recognizes the importance of this principle (Proverbs 28:13; Galatians 6:1-3; James 5:16).

Here are some guidelines for completing your Fifth Step.[5]

With Yourself:

- Writing your Fourth Step inventory began the process. Now set an empty chair across from you with an imaginary double of yourself in it, or sit in front of a mirror so you can see yourself speak. Talk out loud using your Fourth Step inventory as your guide. Allow yourself time to hear what you are saying and note any deeper understandings.

With God:
- Start with prayer. Thank Him for listening and for His gift of love and grace. Ask Him for direction and to remove the fear. Tell God about your inventory. Confess your faults and sin and ask for forgiveness. Then thank Him in the name of Jesus Christ.
- Speak out loud, sincerely and honestly sharing your inventory. Present both your strengths and weaknesses.

With another person:
- Choose your listener carefully. The individual can be a pastor, trusted friend, counselor, doctor, family member, or member of a Twelve Step program.
- Begin with prayer, calling upon Christ to be present and to give support and guidance.
- Allow ample time to complete your thoughts. Stick pretty much to your inventory unless a new insight comes to you.
- Eliminate distractions. No phone calls or family interruptions.
- The goal is to admit the exact nature of your wrongs. It is not necessary to discuss how the wrongs came about or how changes will be made. This is not a counseling session.
- The listener is to be patient and accepting, asking questions to help you express your thoughts clearly, and above all, observing confidentiality.
- After Step Five is completed, both of you can share your feelings about the experience. This is an opportunity to extend the love of God to each other.

STEP SIX
Be entirely ready to have God remove all these defects of character (James 4:10).

In Step Six we become ready to have God remove the defects of character which were uncovered earlier. Here we are confronted with the need to change our attitudes and lifestyles. The changes that will take place in our lives come from a cooperative effort. God provides the direction and enabling power. We provide the willingness. God will lead if we let Him. He never forces Himself on us. We must invite Him into our lives, content in knowing that He will never leave or forsake us.[6]

We cannot be totally free from defects, but God can work through our imperfections. However, we must be willing to be free of them. Step Six is not an action step so much as it is a state of readiness to release our faults to God. As our willingness to surrender increases, God is able to remove our defects as He sees fit. Once again we are confronted with the dangerous nature of our self-will. It has never been enough to help us. This step encourages us to relinquish our self-destructive nature and move on with hope.

- Explain your commitment to allowing your behavior to be changed. What are you willing to do to change?
- Read Psalm 37:4-5 and 1 Peter 1:13-14. What do these verses say about the requirements for change?
- What if you are afraid to let go of your defects? Read Deuteronomy 31:8; Joshua 1:9; Isaiah 41:10. What can happen to your fear?
- Read Psalm 119:10-12 and James 1:5-6; 4:10. What part do the Word of God, humility, and truth play in your recovery?
- Consider pride, greed, lust, dishonesty, anger, gluttony, envy, and laziness one at a time. List personal examples of each and consider what will be involved in giving up that defect.

STEP SEVEN
Humbly ask Him to remove our shortcomings (1 John 1:9).

Asking God to remove our shortcomings is a true measure of our willingness to surrender control. The key concept in the step is *humility.* We are humble because we recognize our need and God's ability to meet that need. We are humble because we understand that we do nothing to deserve or earn His loving gifts to us. In our humility, we make ourselves receptive to His help.[7]

Step Seven is the first and most important part of the cleansing process and prepares us for the next stage of our journey. The first six steps allowed us to become aware of our desperate situation and our need for change. Step Seven presents us with the opportunity to turn to God again and ask for removal of those behaviors and attitudes that cause pain.

Preparing to have our defects removed requires our willingness to work with God to revise and redirect our attention and activities. We must ever be vigilant and alert to the possible return of old habits.

We must also realize God gives grace through many channels. He can use other people and situations to bring about change. Pastors, teachers, doctors, and therapists can all be instruments of God's grace. Our willingness to seek outside help can be a clear indication of our readiness to change. A relationship addict or anorexic can pray to God for help with compulsions, as well as seek treatment from a professional counselor.

- What do you learn about humility from these verses: Proverbs 16:18-19; 22:4; 29:23; Isaiah 57:15; Romans 12:3; James 4:6-10; 1 Peter 5:6?
- What are the promises to the humble found in these verses: Matthew 5:3; 18:4; Luke 14:10-11?
- What are one or two outward signs that represent humility? (i.e., a willingness to go down on your knees before God)

STEP EIGHT
Make a list of all persons we have harmed, and be willing to make amends to them all (Luke 6:31).

Prior to recovery, many of us blamed everybody else for our problems. We probably even blamed God. In Step Eight, we begin to release our need to blame others for our misfortune and, instead, accept full responsibility for our own lives. Our Fourth Step inventory revealed that our inappropriate actions caused injury to ourselves and others. Now we must prepare to accept full responsibility and make amends.

This step will improve our relationships with ourselves and others, and help us overcome isolation and loneliness. As we continue to welcome Christ's presence into our hearts, we will develop a new openness with others that will prepare us for the honest admission of our past misconduct.

Here we examine each past misdeed and identify the persons involved. Our intention is to make amends in order to heal our past so God can transform the present.[8]

Forgiveness is an important part of this step. It involves canceling a debt (Matthew 18:23-27). Forgiveness has three expressions. We are to ask God for forgiveness when we sin (1 John 1:9). We are to ask forgiveness from others when we offend them (James 5:16). And we are to grant forgiveness to others when they have sinned against us (Matthew 6:14-15; Ephesians 4:32; Colossians 3:13).

Forgiving others, and asking forgiveness from God and man, helps us approach our recovery free from the resentments and guilt of the past. Forgiveness does not change the past, nor is forgetting a requirement. Rather, we are to give up the right to seek revenge for past wrongs committed against us, and ask others if they will do the same.

- Start by reviewing your Step Four inventory to see who belongs on your list. Record the harm you think you have caused. While doing this, try to sustain thoughts and actions of reconciliation.
- What feelings arise while making your list? Are there issues of forgiveness remaining? What are they?
- Here are three categories in which you may have caused harm. Consider each one in terms of *who* you harmed, *what* you did, and its *effect* on yourself and others. In Step Nine you will seek out the people you have harmed and make amends wherever necessary. For now, all you need to do is list them and describe the consequences.[9]

Material wrongs: Actions which affected an individual in a tangible way. These might include:
  - Inappropriate use of money
  - Refusing to abide by a contract or promise
  - Injuring persons or property.

Moral wrongs: Inappropriate behavior in moral or ethical actions and conduct, including questions of rightness or fairness. The principal issue is involving others in our wrongdoing.
  - Setting a bad example

- Being preoccupied with selfish pursuits and unresponsive to the needs of others
- Forgetting important events such as birthdays of family members
- Inflicting moral harm through infidelity, broken promises, abuse, lack of trust, or lying.

Spiritual wrongs: Acts of omission that result from neglecting our obligations to God, ourselves, and family and community.
- Making no effort to fulfill your obligations and showing no gratitude toward others who have helped you
- Avoiding self-development
- Being inattentive to others in your life.

STEP NINE

Make direct amends to such people wherever possible, except when to do so would injure them or others (Matthew 5:23-24).

In Step Eight we made the list; in Step Nine we actually make amends. We go to the people we have hurt to acknowledge our wrongdoing and to ask forgiveness. This fulfills our requirement to reconcile with others.

Good judgment, a careful sense of timing, courage, and stamina are the qualities needed in this step. Making amends will release us from many resentments of the past, and remove our guilt.

Some people may feel bitter toward us. They may feel threatened by us and resent our changed behavior. It is important to pray about the appropriateness of facing each person directly. We need God's direction before any action is taken.

It is easy to procrastinate by saying, "The time is not yet right." We can find endless excuses. We can rationalize that our past can't be changed, so we should let bygones be bygones. We need to honestly admit that fear and pride are our stumbling blocks. We lack courage when we need it. At this point we should humble ourselves before God again and ask for the courage to do that which is necessary to lay our past to rest.[10]

Step Nine has two distinct parts. The first is making direct amends to people. The second is not to make contact, because it would cause more harm.

Make direct amends when possible. There are two alternatives here:

Some people should be approached as soon as possible. These would include family, friends, creditors, coworkers, and others with whom we can talk. We are to be direct, honest, straightforward, and brief, clearly identifying what we have done wrong, taking full responsibility for our behavior, expressing our remorse, and asking forgiveness.

If long distances are involved, phone calls are helpful. Letter writing should be used as a last resort. It's too hard to get feedback and tends to minimize the effect of the process. The difficulty of the face-to-face encounter shows the listener how much we value him or her and the restoration of the relationship.[11]

In some cases it will not be possible to make amends. We can't locate the people or they have died. In this instance, prayer, writing a letter as if the person were to receive it, or asking some neutral person to hear your statement on the offended person's behalf may help. We can also make amends by performing a kindness for someone else. We can even give restitution to a person who is in some way connected to the one we have harmed (1 Peter 4:8-10).

Except when it would injure. In some situations, we can make only partial restitution because complete disclosure could cause more harm or pain.

Such cases could involve loss of employment, legal action, or threat to one's family. We need to weigh the options carefully. When we choose to delay merely out of fear for ourselves, we are the ones to suffer. If, indeed, there is possibility of causing injury to others through our act of confession, we are acting appropriately to find another way to make amends.

In cases where our own pain or the pain of the offended party is recent and intense, we should be very cautious, and might do well to seek outside counsel.[12]

- Who on your amends list causes you the most concern? What do you think you should do about that situation? Read: Hebrews 12:1; Matthew 18:15; Mark 11:24-25.
- Develop a plan for meeting with each person on your list.
- Decide the priority order and then follow your plan.

STEP TEN
Continue to take personal inventory and, when we were wrong, promptly admit it (1 Corinthians 10:12).

In this step we begin the maintenance segment of the steps. The first nine steps put our house in order and enabled us to change some of our destructive behavior patterns. Now we continue the process of self-examination begun in Step Four. However, this time the focus is on the present. We try to identify and take responsibility for any wrong thoughts, speech, or behavior which could threaten current relationships. We are coming to know the joy of living in harmony with others, free from guilt and fear, and we don't want to slip back into our old ways.[13]

The temptation is to relax, get sloppy about our commitment, and revert back to our old bravado. We must recognize that success will be maintained only if all elements of our recovery are practiced daily.

A *personal inventory* is a daily examination of our strengths and weaknesses, motives and behaviors. We need to monitor signs of attempting to manage our lives without God or of slipping into resentment, dishonesty, or selfishness. When we see these temptations arising, we are to take immediate action. If we have made poor choices or committed a sin, we need to ask God to forgive us and make amends. The key here is promptness. We should settle differences as quickly as possible (Matthew 5:25-26), making confession as soon as we are aware of the failure.

Daily practice of Step Ten maintains our honesty and humility and allows continued sobriety. Taking regular inventory makes us less inclined to yield to old habits. It is a way of centering in on our relationship with God. It can be a form of meditation and communion with God that enriches our spiritual life.

There are three types of inventories: Spot-Check Inventory, Daily Inventory, and Long-Term Periodic Inventory.

Spot-check inventory. Stop for a few moments several times each day to analyze what is happening. It can be a short review of actions, thoughts, and motives. It is a tool for examining each situation, to see what we are doing right and wrong, and to take prompt corrective action wherever necessary.

Daily inventory. This is a day-end review of what has happened. It is a chance to examine our involvements, look at our choices, and prepare a balance sheet of the positive and negative opportunities. We can thank God for helping us with the things that went right, and confess to Him our failures on things that went wrong. The inventory also serves to remind ourselves that we are on a daily journey to recovery. We can never lose sight of the one-day-at-a-time process.

If there is a relapse of some type, we need to avoid all-or-nothing thinking. We fell. That is a reality. But tomorrow is a new opportunity to lay hold of God and, with His help, make it a successful day.

Long-term periodic inventory. This can be accomplished by being alone or going away for a time. These can be special days set aside for reflecting on our lives in solitude or by attending a retreat.

Such an inventory done once or twice a year gives a chance to reflect on our progress from a clearer perspective.

A commitment to taking personal inventory and acting on it promptly will free us to complete the final two steps and obtain the freedom and serenity God wishes for us.[14]

- Take a moment right now and complete a spot-check inventory.
- What did you observe?
- Describe a recent situation where you were wrong and promptly admitted it.
- Read: Psalm 139:23-24; Romans 6:1-4; Galatians 6:1-5; 2 Timothy 3:14. What do these verses say to you in regard to this step?

STEP ELEVEN
Seek through prayer and meditation to improve our conscious contact with God as we understand Him, praying for knowledge of His will for us and the power to carry that out (Colossians 3:16a).

Step Eleven is our opportunity to develop a deepening relationship with God the Father. We do this through prayer and meditation, to improve our conscious contact with Him as well as to become more sensitive and responsive to His guidance.

This daily regimen of prayer and meditation makes it clear that relief from pains of the past is a day-to-day reprieve. Recovery must be relentlessly pursued on a daily basis.[15]

Praying for knowledge of God's will for us and for the

power to carry it out helps us set aside our self-serving motives. Prayer also gives us access to the gifts of His answers. "Therefore I tell you, whatever you ask for in prayer, believe that you have received it, and it will be yours. And when you stand praying, if you hold anything against anyone, forgive him, so that your Father in heaven may forgive you your sins" (Mark 11:24).

Meditation enables us to become better acquainted with God in the same way we become acquainted with a good friend. We spend time together. In the act of meditating, we recall, ponder, and apply our knowledge of God's ways, purposes, and promises. It is an activity of holy thought consciously performed in the presence of God. Its purpose is to clear our mental and spiritual vision and let His truth make its full and proper impact on our minds and hearts. Meditation humbles us as we contemplate God's greatness and glory and allow His Spirit to encourage, reassure, and comfort us.

If we are progressing, we will see signs along the way. We will feel more at peace in our daily affairs, and will experience gratitude for the ongoing healing of compulsive behavior. We will have a sense of identity as children of God. We know we have a rightful place in the world. Feelings of worth will replace feelings of shame.[16]

- How do you think God will respond to your attempts to draw closer to Him? Read: Proverbs 8:17; Jeremiah 29:13; 33:3; Hosea 6:3.
- How do you think you will know if God is listening? (1 John 5:14-15)
- Take some time to get quiet before God in a place where you can meditate and pray. What are your reactions?

STEP TWELVE
Having had a spiritual awakening as the result of these steps, we try to carry this message to others, and to practice these principles in all our affairs (Galatians 6:1).

This step encompasses the joy of a compulsion conquered, and the responsibility of sharing the process. The journey thus far has brought pain and joy as we struggled to turn loose of old habits and ways of thinking. With each day of success there was cause to celebrate and praise God.

With each day of failure there was pain, and a need to confess and seek God. Every journey has milestones or markers. Our recovery has left some markers along the way. There are buckets of tears, shouts of joy, screams for help, and words of celebration.

Step Twelve doesn't mean we have arrived. It means we have undergone a transformation from a compulsion-driven being to one who has found the freedom of spirit promised by God. The journey has shown us that humility gives us power through God, and obedience gives us freedom. Together they release us from the attachment to a mood-altering experience. We are still wearing the same skin, but things are becoming different. We have a greater appreciation of the truly important things in life. We are beginning to understand the kingdom of God.

Our spiritual awakening brings us peace. Life will not be trouble free; problems will abound. There will be times of confusion and doubt and pain will surround us like a band of thorns. But our sense of God's presence will give us peace in spite of our problems. No longer will we need to escape to our addiction. With God as our resource, no problem need be overwhelming.

The resources in our community of supportive friends and family, along with the understandings gained from the steps, will give us strength.

We have seen how God has used our suffering in a redemptive way. Our pain brought us to Him. For that we can be eternally grateful.

Our gratitude motivates us to help others. We are instructed to bring the Good News to all who will hear (Romans 10:14-15). This is the action portion of this step. It is far more effective to witness a principle being applied than to listen to words alone. The best way to convey the power of our spiritual journey is to live the principled life free from compulsive behavior and centered on God. Through our sharing about the transformed life in Jesus Christ, we can help pass along the good news of both God's saving grace and a redemptive healing.

- Write out or create a form of celebration and joy! It can be in any manner or format you wish. Express your feelings about the gift of freedom from compulsion.

- How might you describe your current spiritual awareness?
- Read Titus 3:3-7. How does this relate to your journey?
- What are some ways you can share your version of the Good News with someone else? Brainstorm some ideas and pick a couple to try this week.

This concludes our discussion of the journey through the Twelve Steps. I hope that you feel encouraged that there is a structure for overcoming your compulsion. Others have been exactly where you are and have emerged victorious. The struggle is enormous, but God is bigger than any battle. He wants you to have a victorious life.

Join us, won't you? We're here to walk you through the process. The steps are not an end in themselves. To think so would be to trade one addiction for another. God has used this process very effectively and He can help you also. God is with you.

N O T E S

1. William Lenters, *The Freedom We Crave* (Grand Rapids: Eerdmans), 1985, 115.
2. C.S. Lewis, *The Voyage of the Dawn Treader* (New York: Collier Books), 1952, 93.
3. Friends in Recovery, *The Twelve Steps for Christians* (San Diego: Recovery Publications), 1988, 12–13.
4. Margery Williams, *The Velveteen Rabbit* (New York: Doubleday & Co.), 1971, 16–17.
5. Friends in Recovery, *The Twelve Steps for Christians*, 57–60.
6. *Ibid.*, 61.
7. Claire W., *God, Help Me Stop*, (San Diego: Books West), 1985, 45.
8. Friends in Recovery, *The Twelve Steps for Christians*, 75–76.
9. *Ibid.*, 82.
10. *Ibid.*, 85–86.
11. Claire W., *God, Help Me Stop*, 55.
12. Friends in Recovery, *The Twelve Steps for Christians*, 91.
13. Claire W., *God, Help Me Stop*, 59.
14. Friends in Recovery, *The Twelve Steps for Christians*, 97–101.
15. *Ibid.*, 104.
16. *Ibid.*, 106–107.

RESOURCE AGENCIES

Al-Anon Family Group Headquarters
World Service Office
P.O. Box 182, Madison Square Station
New York, NY 10159-0182

Al-Anon Family Group Headquarters
1372 Broadway
(at 38th Street)
7th Floor
New York, NY 10018
800-245-4656
212-302-7240
(in New York area)

Alcoholics Anonymous
P.O. Box 459
Grand Central Station
New York, NY 10163
212-536-8026

Alcoholics Anonymous
National Headquarters
Box 459
Grand Central Station
New York, NY 10161
212-686-1100

Alcoholics Anonymous
General Services Office (AA)
468 Park Avenue South
New York, NY 10016
212-686-1100

*Alcoholics for Christ, Inc.
1316 North Campbell Road
Royal Oak, MI 48067
313-399-9955

*Alcoholics Victorious
International Service Office
1700 Eighth Street
Lewiston, ID 83501

Anorexia Nervosa and Related Eating Disorders, Inc.
Box 5102
Eugene, OR 97405
503-344-1144

Anorexia/Bulimia Treatment and Education Center
621 South New Ballas Road
Suite 7019B
St. Louis, MO 63141
1-800-222-2832

Bulimia/Anorexia Self-Help (BASH)
522 North New Ballas Road
St. Louis, MO 63141
314-567-4040

Bulimia Anorexia Self-Help, Inc.
6125 Clayton Avenue
Suite #215
St. Louis, MO 63139
1-800-227-4785

Children of Alcoholics Foundation, Inc.
200 Park Avenue, 31st Floor
New York, NY 10166
212-949-1404

*Christian Alcoholics Rehabilitation Association
FOA Road
Pocahontas, MS 39072

Co-Sex Addicts (Co-SA)
Twin Cities Co-S.A.
P.O. Box 14537
Minneapolis, MN 55414
612-537-6904

Emotional Health Anonymous
World Service Office
2420 San Gabriel Blvd.
Rosemead, CA 91770
818-573-5482
213-283-3574

*Exodus International
P.O. Box 2121
San Rafael, CA 94912
415-454-1017

Gamblers Anonymous
National Service Office
P.O. Box 17173
Los Angeles, CA 90017
213-386-8789

Gamblers Anonymous
National Council on
Compulsive Gambling
444 West 56th Street,
Room 3207S
New York, NY 10019
212-765-3833

Help Anorexia, Inc.
5143 Overland Avenue
Culver City, CA 90230
213-837-5445
213-836-1191

Homosexuals Anonymous
P.O. Box 7881
Redding, PA 19603
800-253-3000
215-376-1146

**Incest Survivors
Anonymous**
P.O. Box 5613
Long Beach, CA 90805

***Institute for Christian
Living**
Riverside Medical Center
Minneapolis, MN 55427
612-593-1791

*Liontamers
2801 North Brea Blvd.
Fullerton, CA 92635-2799

Narcotics Anonymous
World Service Office
16155 Wyandotte Street
Van Nuys, CA 91406
818-780-3951

Narcotics Anonymous
World Service Office
P.O. Box 9999
Van Nuys, CA 91409
818-780-3951

**National Anorexic
Aid Society**
5796 Carl Road
Columbus, OH 43229
614-436-1112

**National Association for
Children of Alcoholics**
31706 Coast Highway
Suite 201
South Laguna, CA 92677
714-499-3889

**National Association of
Anorexia Nervosa and
Associated Disorders, Inc.**
Box 271
Highland Park, IL 60035
708-831-3438

**National Institute of
Drug Abuse Prevention
Branch**
5600 Fishers Lane,
Room 10A-30
Rockville, MD 20852
800-662-4357

**National Self-Help
Clearing House**
33 West 42nd Street
New York, NY 10036
212-840-1259

*New Life Treatment Center
P.O. Box 38
Woodstock, MN 56186

*Overcomers Outreach, Inc.
2290 West Whittier Blvd.,
Suite D
LaHabra, CA 90631
213-697-3994

Overeaters Anonymous
P.O. Box 92870
Los Angeles, CA 90009
213-320-7941

Parents Anonymous
National Office
6733 South Sepulveda Blvd.
Suite 270
Los Angeles, CA 90045
800-421-0353

Parents United
Daughters and Sons
United
Adults Molested as
Children United
P.O. Box 952
San Jose, CA 95108
409-280-5055

S-Anon
P.O. Box 5117
Sherman Oaks, CA
91413
818-990-6910

Sex Addicts Anonymous
(SAA)
P.O. Box 3038
Minneapolis, MN 55403
612-871-1520

Sex and Love Addicts
Anonymous (SLAA)
Augustine Fellowship
P.O. Box 119
New Town Branch
Boston, MA 02258

Sexaholics Anonymous (SA)
P.O. Box 300
Simi Valley, CA 93062

SpenderMenders
P.O. Box 15000-156
San Francisco, CA 94115
415-775-9754

*Substance Abusers
Victorious
One Cascade Plaza
Akron, OH 44308

Victims Anonymous (VA)
9514-9 Roseda Blvd. #607
Northridge, CA 91324
813-993-1139

*Designates resource with Christian orientation.

RECOMMENDED BOOKS

1. William Backus and Marie Chapian, *Telling Yourself the Truth* (Minneapolis: Bethany House), 1980.

2. Melody Beattie, *Codependent No More* (New York: Hazelden), 1987.

3. David Burns, *Feeling Good* (New York: New American Library), 1980.

4. Patrick Carnes, *Out of the Shadows* (Minneapolis: CompCare Publishers), 1983.

5. Claire W., *God, Help Me Stop* (San Diego: Books West), 1985.

6. Cheryl Forbes, *The Religion of Power* (Grand Rapids: Zondervan), 1983.

7. Richard Foster, *Celebration of Discipline* (San Francisco: Harper & Row), 1978.

8. Richard Foster, *Money, Sex & Power* (San Francisco: Harper & Row), 1985.

9. Friends in Recovery, *The Twelve Steps—A Spiritual Journey* (San Diego: Recovery Publications), 1988.

10. Friends in Recovery, *The Twelve Steps for Christians* (San Diego: Recovery Publications), 1988.

11. Howard Halpern, *How to Break Your Addiction to a Person* (New York: Bantam Books), 1982.

12. Tim Hansel, *When I Relax I Feel Guilty* (Elgin, Illinois: David C. Cook), 1979.

13. Archibald Hart, *Adrenaline & Stress* (Waco, Texas: Word Books), 1988.

14. Judi Hollis, *Fat Is a Family Affair* (San Francisco: Hazelden), 1985.

15. Kevin Leman, *The Pleasers* (Old Tappan, New Jersey: Fleming Revell), 1987.

16. William Lenters, *The Freedom We Crave* (Grand Rapids: Wm. B. Eerdmans), 1985.

17. Grant Martin, *Counseling for Family Violence and Abuse* (Waco, Texas: Word Books), 1987.

18. Grant Martin, *Please Don't Hurt Me* (Wheaton, Illinois: Victor Books), 1987.

19. Grant Martin, *Transformed by Thorns* (Wheaton, Illinois: Victor Books), 1985.

20. Gerald May, *Addiction and Grace* (New York: Harper & Row), 1988.

21. Keith Miller, *SIN: Overcoming the Ultimate Deadly Addiction* (San Francisco: Harper & Row), 1987.

22. Philip Parham, *Letting God: Christian Meditations for Recovering Persons* (San Francisco: Harper & Row), 1987.

23. Anne Wilson Schaef, *Escape from Intimacy* (New York: Harper & Row), 1989.

24. Sandra Simpson LeSourd, *The Compulsive Woman* (Old Tappan, New Jersey: Fleming H. Revell), 1987.

25. Anderson Spickard and Barbara Thompson, *Dying for a Drink* (Waco, Texas: Word Books), 1985.

26. Steven VanCleave, Walter Byrd and Kathy Revell, *Counseling for Substance Abuse and Addiction* (Waco, Texas: Word Books), 1987.

27. Raymond Vath, *Counseling Those with Eating Disorders* (Waco, Texas: Word Books), 1986.

28. Richard Walters, *Counseling for Problems of Self-Control* (Waco, Texas: Word Books), 1987.

You may contact the author at the following address:

Dr. Grant L. Martin
CRISTA Counseling Service
19303 Fremont Ave. N.
Seattle, Washington 98133
206-546-7215